AF365733

MAKE EM BELIEVE IT

Tom Arild Fjeld

Foreword by Tom Arild Fjeld

The most important thing for a Christian, who shares what he thinks he stands for. Is that he believes what he says and serves his fellow human beings. If one does not believe what one stands for, it is only a religious exercise one has. When you come forth as a witness, people should be able to look at you and experience the faith in what you preach flowing out of you.

What I give in this book is my experience of God's Word in this area. I want the book to be an instruction book, a training book, and a guide book for you. I want it to be a book that teaches you to live with the infectious effect of faith. I want you to make all your listeners believe everything you proclaim.

When the conviction of the Word of God lives strong in you, you will automatically proclaim it with power and heaviness. People see you believe it and it will spread to the audience. You make them believe the same as you believe.

Chapter Alpha and Omega

God's plan of action for you

The absolute realities of a born-again, surrendered, obedient believer in Christ

Biblical evangelism

This is the biblical way of evangelizing, there is no other. The costume of evangelism may be different, but the essence and message are just one thing, the work of the Atonement of Jesus Christ on Calvary. That is what I show from the Bible here.

Music in use in evangelism

It will also be completely wrong if it does not have the expansive core message contained in the song proclamation. It should be the music of victory, the music of war that is spiritual. If not, it is only religious music (lifeless), the same as speech without the expansive core message itself.

Spirituality

Spirituality cannot be provoked or "left" as one has. If you are spiritual in Christ, it will be an automatic authority in your life that is discovered by everyone, even if they do not know what it is. You will always be revealed, it will appear on and off you whether you are religious or a spiritual believer in Jesus. One who lives a surrendered and consecrated life through the Bible to Jesus. A core verse in this context is:

"Jesus said, If you abide in me and my words abide in you, pray for what you will, and you will receive it." (John. 15: 7)

Christ's Commandment to All of Us - The Missionary Command - The Evangelization Commandment

"And Jesus said to the disciples, go into all the world (Cosmos, Greek, and Hebrew) and preach the gospel to all creation!

He who believes and is baptized will be saved, but he who does not believe will be condemned.

And these signs will follow them like tyrants, in my name, they will cast out evil spirits. They must speak with tongues.

They will take snakes in their hands, and if they drink deadly poison, it will not harm them. In sick they shall lay their hands, and they shall be healed. " (Mark. 16, 15-18)

"When Jesus was with them, he commanded them not to leave Jerusalem, but to wait for what the Father had promised, that which, he said, you heard from me.

For John baptized with water, but ye shall be baptized with the Holy Ghost not many days henceforth.

You will have power (Divine power in motion) in the Holy Spirit coming upon you. And you shall be my witnesses (Martyrs, Greek proof-makers, Norwegian) both in Jerusalem and throughout Judea and Samaria and just to the ends of the earth (the outermost and most distant regions).

When he had said this, he was lifted up as they watched, and a cloud took him away from their eyes. " (Acts. 1.4-5 and 8-9)

"Then, after speaking this to them, the Lord Jesus was taken to heaven, and sat down at the right hand of God.

But the disciples preached everywhere. And the Lord worked with and confirmed the Word (the work of Jesus Christ on Calvary, Bible promises and commands) by the signs that came. "
(Mark. 16: 19-20)

"The disciples asked Jesus: What shall we do to do the works of God?
Jesus answered and said unto them, this is the work of God, that ye should believe on that which God hath sent. (John 6, 28-29)

Our call from heaven is to believe in Christ and obey Him. If we do that, our faith and the exercise of His will, will increase with strength and power in our lives as He wills.

The absolute realities of a born-again, surrendered, obedient believer in Christ.

A core verse in this context is:
"Jesus said, If you abide in me and my words

abide in you, pray for what you will, and you will receive it." (John 15: 7)

Christ's Commandment to UsAll - The Missionary Command - The Evangelization Commandment

"And Jesus said to the disciples, Go into all the world (Cosmos, Greek, and Hebrew) and preach the gospel to all creation!

He who believes and is baptized will be saved (saved; but he who does not believe will be condemned.

And these signs will follow them like tyrants, In my name they will cast out evil spirits. They must speak with tongues.

They will take snakes in their hands, and if they drink deadly poison, it will not harm them. In sick they shall lay their hands, and they shall be healed." (Mark. 16, 15-18)

"When Jesus was with them, he commanded them not to leave Jerusalem, but to wait for what the Father had promised, that which, he said, you heard from me.

For John baptized with water, but ye shall be baptized with the Holy Ghost not many days henceforth.

You will have power (Divine power in motion) in the Holy Spirit coming upon you. And you shall be my witnesses (Martyrs, Greek proof-makers, Norwegian) both in Jerusalem and throughout Judea and Samaria and just to the ends of the earth (the outermost and most distant regions).

When he had said this, he was lifted up as they watched, and a cloud took him away from their eyes. " (Acts 1.4-5 and 8-9)

"Then, after speaking this to them, the Lord Jesus was taken to heaven, and sat down at the right hand of God.

But the disciples preached everywhere. And the Lord worked with and confirmed the Word (the work of Jesus Christ on Calvary, Bible promises

and commands) by the signs that came."
(Mark 16: 19-20)

"The disciples asked Jesus: What shall we do to
do the works of God?
Jesus answered and said unto them, this is the
work of God, that ye should believe on that
which God hath sent. (John 6, 28-29)

Our call from heaven is and believe in Christ to
obey Him. If we do that, our faith and the exercise of His will will increase with strength and
power in our lives as He wills.

**You are a messenger of God in the place of
Christ with power**

"Then we are messengers in Christ's place, as if
God himself exhorted us. We pray in the place of
Christ: Be reconciled to God. " (2 Cor 5: 20)

"I will make you a light unto the Gentiles, that
my salvation may be too the ends of the earth."
(Isa.49, 6)

"For we know that all things work together for the good of those who love God, those who are called according to his counsel." (Rom. 8, 28)

"For every one that calleth on the name of the Lord shall be saved.

But how can they call on someone they have not come to believe in? And how can they believe in someone they haven't heard of? And how can they hear without anyone preaching?

And how can they preach without being sent out "As it is written, How beautiful are their feet that bring peace, that bring good tidings!"
(Rom. 10, 13-15)

You have been given everything in Christ - It is Christ's command for you to bring it out alive with the power of the Holy Spirit.

Foreword by Morris Cerullo

It is with great humility and I consider it a great honor to write this foreword. Pastor Tom is the quintessential leader; a man after the heart of God, a man with a great calling, a man full of God's word and power, a great intercessor and a faithful soldier for Christ.

His books were born out of a divinely inspired spirit deeply rooted in the Holy Scriptures, the Bible, the Word of God. Part of the devil's strategy is that he will cause us to live a poor life in defeat by neglecting the study of God's Word daily. That is why God has placed these great words in Pastor Tom to help His children gain more knowledge of Him and His kingdom.

The power comes from what you know and how you can use what you know to help you, in opening up the revelation, guidance, and inspiration of the Holy Spirit. Follow Pastor Tom as he takes you on spiritual training sessions, on the spiritual training studio.

You will be encouraged to believe God for the impossible. These books are a must for any believer who has an insurmountable desire to move and live on the next level. You will get yourself aroused, to delve deeper into what is of God.

Pastor. Dr. Morris Cerullo

CONTENTS

1

A world in turmoil

Look around the world, what does media write about, what does media display on TV. There is nothing but turmoil, rebellion, war, terror and murder in all variants.

The human mind has been overflowing with Satan's thoughts. Mankind has accepted Satan's thoughts as his own and identifies himself with them. This has bombarded us since we were young children in all their varieties.

Believe Satan's thoughts/words

Man thinks Satan's thoughts and ideas are their own thoughts and ideas.

This is an area unknown to most people. For a natural unborn human, this is an area unattainable.

The reborn has the opportunity to gain the knowledge they need in the spiritual world.

Man grabs one of Satan's thoughts that come to them and believes it strongly. They act on it, they put it into action in their lives. Thoughts in their minds become a reality in the physical world.

It works
Faith in action on Satan's words works.

Mankind has created its own world through spiritual thoughts and words. Every thought gives a feeling and every feeling gives a thought. Every emotion is turned into words in a human brain. Spiritual words have brought forth everything we see around us. Mankind has built its own world on the earth with thoughts from the spiritual world.

Everything is guided by the thoughts you receive

Every religion, every terrorist organization, every political leadership, yes everything we see on earth, is a result of thought. Satan gives different thoughts completely to different people, to put peoples and nations against each other. Man is like helpless "puppets in Satan's mind".

Helpless victims

The man on earth believes that every thought
that comes to them is their own product.
They work from their thoughts in everything
they do. They do not think that thoughts must
come from somewhere. They think they're just
there, they're just coming. Man believes in ideas,
new gains, inventions, they believe everything is
just there in the brain. It thinks that's just the
way it is.

Imagine being seduced that way.

Do you think that just so, you are caught in Satan's mind, without knowing it? Many have also
been given the idea that tells them, Satan can't
find. They also believe this strongly. That God
does not exist they believe even stronger. What
are you left with then? You have left yourself, a
helpless victim on planet earth, with no hope and
future. You have truly become a helpless victim.
You are on this planet floating in space. You
have no chance to jump off. You must stay on
this planet until you die. And what then?

4

Adam and Eve's choices

God gave them their own free will. God is love,
He would choose them even if they would obey
Him. In the first use of free will, they violated
God's command, God's law.
The only thing they had left after the fall was the
will to choose. But now they could not correct
what they had chosen wrong. Now they were out
in a sinful world, a world that had broken God's
command to them.

Your gift of love from God

The only thing God gave Adam and Eve was
free will. With that will, they managed to be the
forerunners of a world of "Ragnarok" that we
see today. We still have the will, now it is about
choosing the right, choosing Christ as Lord.

The hardening is going on

"A man who is often punished and yet stiffens
his neck will be broken in an instant, and there is
no cure." (Ecclesiastes 29, 1)

Is this what you want?

Listen to this:

"And the fourth angel poured out his bowl upon the sun, and it had the power to burn people with fire;

And the people burned in severe heat, and they blasphemed the name of God, who has the makings of these plagues, and they did not repent to give him glory.

And the fifth angel poured out his bowl upon the throne of the beast, and its kingdom was darkened, and they chewed their tongues in torment,

And they blasphemed the God of heaven for their torments and their abominations and did not repent of their deeds. " (Rev 16, 8 - 11)

If it is as far as you want it to go, it is not necessary. Put your pride down. Recognize God Jehovah, the self-existent who reveals himself and is eternal. The Creator of all things, humble yourself before Him. The blessing will be part of Him. You will have a happy life.

6

Are you stuck in the screwdriver?

If you are in the Western "enlightened" world, one of those who deny everything you cannot relate to on earth, you only believe in the physical, you are an evolutionist. Which has fallen into self-righteousness and the snare of pride. Or are you one of the many religions of the world, who throughout your life have sought meaning with life. You may have done so through submission of religions or philosophies, but the answer and satisfaction have not been fulfilled.

2

What about all religions

We have gods in all our religions.
Yes, there are gods in all religions, people have always felt the need for something that is their security, god or not god. This has been a reality ever since Adam and Eve.
When security comes one's way, it is seized. We seize the security we can find and keep it.
It is not so dangerous what it is, only it is security.

If you are looking, you will find.
If you are looking for security, you will find security. Whether it is true or false. That's not the most important thing, at least not at first. Eventually, it may be felt that security requires repeat services. Then it's not so nice anymore.

It is the same in religions and politics

Politics seeks solutions and peace; religions seek solutions and peace.

Hear what the Bible says:

With sin, there is no peace.

"There is nothing fresh in my flesh for thy wrath; there is no peace in my bones for my sin." (Psalm 38, 4)

"There is no peace, saith the Lord, to the wicked." (Isa. 48:22)

You see - the inheritance of sin hangs on us like a magnet, it wont loose the grip on you.

The hereditary tragedy is with us today
Mankind had nice progress in life and the generations after Adam and Eve. From that day the sin of inheritance became a reality. Man has always done everything in his power to make peace, it is peace people want, but has always been difficult to achieve as a permanent reality.

In the fullness of time

Listen to what the Bible says. Hear the voice of God that speaks of the restoration of sin's slavery and captivity coming to the fullness of time.

"He must speak peace to the Gentiles,

For the sake of your covenant blood, I will also release your prisoners out of the well of which there is no water. " (Ps 9, 10-11)

"If you do not listen to the voice of your God, then you intend to keep all His commandments and His laws, which I give you today, then all these curses will embrace you and reach you;" (Deut. 28, 15)

"The curse shall follow you until you perish." (Deut. 28:22)

Read the entire chapter. The first 14 verses are about God's rich blessing, the next verses through verse 68, are about the curse.

The day of liberation, from the torture of curse, comes.

3

They don't know what to believe

The first generations of people on earth. Imagine what a difficult situation it was. The story of Adam, Eve, the Garden of Eden and the Fall, was told from generation to generation.

Imagine what grief there was
The vacuum of the fall and loss of the glory and abundance of all that is good lay for man in the "air". The train had left.

Straight out of God's plan
Already the first people had walked right out of God's wonderful plan. Loneliness weighed down, they lived in ignorance of how things were going. The fear lay and the pressure, they felt alone on earth, they longed for what might have been, what they heard.

The spirit of fear in its many degrees of strength came and led the way

The fear does not come first and frightens your life. It comes gently and says something like this: "You probably need to find something that can help you a bit".

A harmless voice, it sounds like a helpful gentle statement, but the tiny little fear is underlying. It is Satan who sets up the course of life for you with fear.

Natural religion

People in the natural religion, like their ancestors, took care of themselves and sacrificed what they gave you shelter and food. They understood that it was important to take care of what gave them what they needed to live. They were afraid, yes, they were afraid that they would not get their daily bread. This led man to begin to satisfy his idols. Such is the nature religion in many parts of the world today as it always has been, the fear lies.

The people of the West

When people in the West hear about possible business closures, many people face problems.

When a family member gets sick, the disease affects the whole family. What happens now? will he be healthy again? The fear lies at the bottom, in different strengths and variants all the way, it strikes where it gets a chance.

Next step worship.

Natural Religion

When we look at the natural religion, we see that the advent of fear has led to worship. In the situation of worship, we see that at one point the ancestors began to experience contact in the spiritual world. This they began to experience because they opened their inner human unconscious to the unknown.

As they began to "indulge" in what gave them daily bread. Then the demons have the opportunity to come on stage. The nature of man believed God as the rescue, had come to them.

Now, the natural religion grew.

In its footsteps, other entirely new religions emerged, some becoming the world's religions. The spirit of fear led this purposefully forward.

Now the religions became the "life" of many nations. Satan had got your man he wants them. Politicians came on the scene, but selfishness was at the forefront, they thought of themselves more than the people they were set to serve. This is how it has continued for centuries to come.

The idols of the West
The West, the Christian part of the world, has its own variety of idols. Of course, it doesn't seem like it's idols, but it's idols. The West doesn't believe in idols, they say it's just fantasy and adventure. Demons, Satan and God do not exist. So far it has come in the "Christian part of the world". Anyway, their own variant of idol worship has the West.
Here are some examples. As I see it, the main idol is the general one.

Materialism
materialism. Under that concept, we have the desire to own as much as possible. Be it houses, estates, cars, boats, food, clothing.

Egoism

Myself, "I" as an idol, selfishness, is also very high on the list today. The Christians also have these idols. These are substitutes for what you should have had, namely a living fellowship with your Creator. Man needs to be "born again" and bring the true God into his life.

When Christ came, a new agenda was set in the world calendar.

Peace with God

God revealed himself by his redeeming name, Jehovah Shalom,

"The Lord our peace" (Judges 6, 22 - 24)

The redemptive blessing of God's peace.

Christ came and paid for our sins for our inheritance.

"The punishment lay upon him, Christ, that we should have peace," (Isa. 53: 5)

"He made peace by his blood on the cross" (Col. 1, 20)

Jesus Christ did not declare us guilty
He did the redeeming work for everyone who
wants to believe it.

Christ redeemed us.

Listen:
"So much more then, after we are justified by
His blood, by Him will we be saved from the
world." (Rom. 5: 9)

"For as many have become sinners by the dis-
obedience of one man, so shall many be justified
by the obedience of one." (Rom 5, 19)

This is what the Bible calls "the gospel of peace"

"How beautiful their feet are that proclaim
peace, that carries good news." (Rom. 10:15)

4

Give them faith in
what you believe

When you explain these truths and people accept Jesus Christ as their savior, Christ Jesus comes into their lives by the Holy Spirit, by the Spirit of God. It's a weird experience, but it's true.

Born again
The peace of Jesus Christ becomes your peace, the life of Jesus Christ becomes your life

"For whom God would make known how rich in glory this secret is among the Gentiles, Christ among them, the hope of glory." (Col. 1, 27)

God set the plan of salvation on our behalf
God knew that if people knew what price his son paid for their salvation, they would respond.

They would be just as eager to make peace with Him as He is to bring them near.
Listen to these Bible verses, they will be opened to you now:

"When he, Jesus did not want anyone to perish, but that all should come to repentance."
(2 Peter 3: 9)

Christ prepared a path of opportunity for us so that we would not perish. He will redeem us from Satan's slavery and restore us to the state in which he had created us to live. So that the peace of Christ might reign in our inner human being.

God sacrificed his son to accomplish this task.

"For God so loved the world that he gave his only begotten Son, that whosoever believeth in him should not perish, but have everlasting life."
(John. 3:16)

God Himself came down to earth but in His Son's body.

Jesus Christ took on all your sin

"He who did not know of sin, Jesus Christ, was made a sin for us, that in him we might become the righteous of God." (2 Cor. 5: 21)

He who was innocent was guilty of you. He took on your guilt, he took on your wrongdoings. Therefore, no violations will be surrendered to us. When he took them, you no longer need them.

"Paul says, He has now reconciled in His mortal body at death, to make you holy and immaculate and unpunished before His face" (Col. 1:22).

Freedom from sin makes you alive

"Even you who were dead by your transgressions and the foreskin of your flesh (here include both Jews and Gentiles), you made him alive with him, forgiving us all our sins.

Wiped out the letter of guilt

And wiped out the letter of guilt against us, which was written with a commandment, taking it away as he nailed it to the cross.

He disarmed the powers and authorities and openly questioned them, proving to be the victorious Lord over them on the cross."
(Col. 2, 13 - 15)

"But now, in Christ Jesus, you, as before, were far away, drawing near to the blood of Christ."
(Eph. 2: 13)

"The punishment for our peace was laid upon Him" (Isa. 53: 5).

"So much more then, after we are justified by the blood of Jesus, by Him we shall be saved from the world." (Rom. 5: 9)

Our sins no longer exist - the mark of sin is gone And by Him, Jesus, He reconciled all things with Him, He took our sins upon Him, Jesus made Himself equal to Yours and My sins, so that we would not have them any longer. You shouldn't have to carry the mark of sin on you anymore.

In the sky

You have now reconciled in His mortal body at death, to make you holy and immaculate and unpunished before His face. " (Col. 1, 19 - 20, 22)

The content of salvation

You no longer need to be afraid of judgment on past sins. Jesus took our punishment. Our past is a debt that is settled, it is paid for. It is erased from our sheet.

This is the content of salvation; this is the truth that creates peace.

The following is what you have to do, you have to do your part of the deal.

Repent and believe the gospel

When you come to Christ with your life and turn around, repent, from your past life. From the sins of your past life, you repent to Christ. You put all the old stuff behind you.

Now you want to live with Jesus as Lord in your life. You will believe Him and follow Him. If you do this seriously, he will welcome you with open arms and give you a whole new life.

You are born again, you become a new creature, you are saved.
The law of sin and evil can no longer control us. You have come into fellowship with God. He has now become your peace. This is something you want to experience in a very specific way. A whole new life in you begins, you are no longer the same. Your body and personality are the same, but your true self, your spirit is brand new. It is sinless, as Adam and Eve's spirit was before the Fall in the Garden of Eden.

"Jesus came with the gospel of God and said:

The time is perfect, and the kingdom of God is near; repent and believe the gospel! "
(Mark 1, 14 - 15)

What a possibility, a whole new life.

Give them faith

Give them faith in what you believe. If you believe it strongly, you are full of inspiration, conviction power and the energy of faith. Now you can stand up and proclaim the gospel alive to those who listen to you. Yes, as a born-again who desires to convey the message of Jesus Christ to others wholeheartedly, make sure you believe it is fighting strongly. If not, it won't work.

Proclaiming style with the power of conviction

God wants you to stand up to explain these truths in a proclaiming style with the power of conviction. Then you will explain it almost poetically. If you do, people will believe it and accept it. They will cheer for joy and clap for convincing enthusiasm.

God has made it easy for us to do this, if only in this position I am talking about.

The basis for receiving the message of grace is God-ordained

I was on a crusade tour of Asia. I had been to Singapore and Malaysia. Now I was on my way to Sri Lanka on India's southern tip. I had come to the city of Gall. I lay on the lawn in the morning, outside where I lived. I was preparing for the evening meeting.

24

Suddenly in a revelation from God, I understood what Proverbs 3, 11 meant.

"He has done all things in his time, and also in eternity he has put in their hearts, but so that man cannot fully understand the work God has done, from beginning to end."
(Ecclesiastes 3, 11)

Recognition factor
Part of eternity is in all people on earth, that's what I now understand. That again made me understand that as I explained, the gospel of Jesus Christ proclaimed strongly in the faith. Then the Holy Spirit, in which I then explained and proclaimed, would be recognized by eternity in the hearts of men. That Spirit in me then hit the recognizing factor of eternity in their hearts. They want to know that what is proclaimed is comfortable and right for them. They are convincingly drawn to it. They know it is liberating and joyful.
Furthermore, I got another word from the Bible that continues that word. It is from Paul's letter to the Ephesians. Let's look at that.

"For by grace are ye saved through faith, and it
is not of yourselves, it is the gift of God"
(Eph. 2: 8)

You can't remove it, it's part of you

We did not have the ability to believe in the message of salvation and salvation by ourselves.
Therefore, God has placed this faith that leads us
to the point of salvation in our hearts. It means
that this opportunity of faith is in all people, no
matter who you are. God has put it there since
you were born. You can't remove it, it's part of
you.

The man walking along the hill, Sri Lanka

I had the crusade in Sri Lanka with great success
for the kingdom of God.
I don't forget the man who couldn't walk. I saw
him out on the street before the first meeting
would begin.
He had no tools, not even a homemade roll plate
that anyone used. He pulled over onto the
ground with his arms. The entire side of the
body, especially the thigh, was with thick skin
like leather.

As I was learning the message of Jesus the first evening, I suddenly saw a man standing by the ropes around the platform, smiling. It was the man who had walked along the hill. Christ had healed him in the meeting, where he stood with his big smile. What a wonderful moment.

The prison

There was a prison with 500 prisoners in Gall, the city where the meetings were to be held. I was asked to come yours and tell about Jesus. When I arrived with my friends from Australia, who were missionaries in Sri Lanka. Relax all the prisoners in the large prison / air yard. The prison guards stood behind and followed. I proclaimed the message of great joy and joy. The prisoners smiled from ear to ear, clapping and cheering. They believed every word I said. All the prisoners were basically Buddhists.

How do prisoners and all other people see Christ? They see Christ in you and me Jehovah God no longer walks on earth in his son's physical body. Christ now sits at the Father's right hand in heaven.

"We have such a high priest who sat on the right side of the throne of the majesty in the heavens," (Heb. 8, 1).

"Christ is the one who is dead, even more so, who is also the resurrection, who is also at God's right hand, who also intercedes for us;" (Rom. 8:34)

Your life is a testimony (proof)
Now God is wandering around and manifesting in His Spirit, the Holy Spirit in Christ in you while He is in heaven. It is all Divine, it is our God Jehovah. Christ's personality, character, and the power of the Holy Spirit's love through you.

Everyone sees what you have and are
You can't fool anyone. Your life is a testimony in your body and your soul / personality. It radiates out of you, good or bad. Make sure Christ seems through you. The fruits of your life and the flowers of the Lord that spring out of you with its smell. The more you see, obviously get these realities, the more Christ will shine through you.

The moment for Salvation were in

After 30 minutes of proclamation style teaching, I invited repentance and salvation in Christ Jesus. They saw the victory, they saw the opportunity All the prisoners throughout the prison would repent to Christ and receive him as their personal savior and Lord. All of them wanted their sins forgiven and cleansed of their sins in the blood of Jesus. Everyone would be born again and become a new creature. I talked and learned until they understood this.

The moment of repentance

The jubilation was most pronounced beyond the possibility of repentance. To put the old life behind its back and forgive. Here they saw the victory immediately.

There were 3 white prisoners in the prison, they were from Europe. They were drug smugglers; they were the only ones who would not surrender their lives to Christ. How many who are preserved in Christ know only heaven, but they all received an opportunity from God who came to their city. My Australian friends had already started work in the city, so now they got a lot of new disciples.

Revelation triumphs in Ahmedabad, India

Furthermore, the crusade went to India, to the city of Amedabad. There were 100,000 people at the meeting on the first evening. Here there was great resistance from the Hindus, Hindu priests were very violent towards the Christians who came.

Now that I had the revelation of the Ecclesiastes 3, 11, and Ephesians 2, 8, my attitude to 100,000 Hindus was different than it had been before. Now I was completely relaxed on the platform. I wasn't looking to convince them of anything. I was not in a warrior position.

The receiver was ready and the transmitter sent

I was there to explain to them in the Spirit of God the simple eternal truths that lead to salvation in Christ, now I knew that the recipient in them was on. My transmitter sent the gospel signals of love.

They didn't understand everything I explained right away. I explained it again. Suddenly the light went up for them. They saw it, they got the revelation from God. The cheers, smiles and applause from the Hindus broke loose. Now it was just harvesting.

Victory's trip gradually went from India to Pakistan and Afghanistan.

Teach, preach and proclaim empathy until they catch it, then they have it.

5

You can never give more than what you have received yourself

Now we see the receivers are clear, even if they don't understand any of that bit themselves. Most people have no understanding of this. We are moving into a whole new existence, a being conscious in the spiritual world on God's part. This is where we come in as God representatives and tools.

Listen to this:

Revelation knowledge given from the world of the Spirit for understanding in the reborn thought life in the physical world

What you see (what is obvious to you) You have
What you have Are you free in
What you are free in What you can give

What you can give Do you have authority over
What you have authority over is yours
What is yours Can you give to whomever you want
What you can give to whom you want Can be received by anyone who wants it
Anyone who wants it See it

What you see - you have

Revelation is nothing that flows by itself within you, as a disciple of Jesus. You have to pay for every little thing you consume. It is only when you have been established at a level in your spiritual life, that you will experience revelation knowledge comes easily and naturally. But as I said, it is a path of suffering to this point. The day you begin to see and understand little by little, things after things in scripture, then you have what you see.

What you have – is what you are free in

An amazing experience to experience. At every point the Lord revives, reveals His word to you, you are free. You move in the freedom you have been given, as you have faith. Understand this.

Let your faith take it

"Jesus said: Whatever you pray with faith in your prayers, you shall receive." (Matt. 21, 22)

"Jesus said: Have faith in God, whatever you say without doubt (Greek, diacrino, discriminate, withdraw, oppose), but believe that what he says, receives it, will receive it.

Therefore, I say to you: Whatever you ask for and desire, just believe that you have received it, it will be revived (Greek Lambano, take in and hold, movement in receiving, seizing, without any reservation) you : "(Mark. 11, 23-24)

Say it and then act it

Tell yourself, when the belief in what you have received is there, say I have it and then act on it. Understand this. If Christ has given you, then act. Tear yourself away from everything that is needed, tear yourself apart, believe yourself free, understand this.

What you are free in – is what you can give

Now you come up with an area in which you are free. You are moving in the authority of love in this area. Everyone sees it and everyone wants to experience it through you. Let all your senses be involved in your proclamation. Only 10 percent of what you say is fixed in humans, the rest is your body speaking to the senses of the audience. Move-in your freedom. Release the poet, the lyricist in you.

"Preach the Word of God in the Synagogue of the Jews" (Acts. 13, 5)

Preacher, Kerugma From Greek, means to illustrate, tone strength and movement are important,

Poetry

We proclaim in a translation from Greek that the word "poetry", poetry which in turn translated from Greek means to bring forth, through imagination, through performing plays. In James 1, 22 "the doers of the word", this word "doers" of the Greek poets, means, in particular, a doer, get on the light, exercise, complete, proclaim, erect. There are many more words that refer to Greek. The ones I have mentioned probably show us enough.

Lyric

Lyric, which is a sibling word for poetry, means to express a feeling spontaneously.

We see clearly that expressing spiritual life and its emotions through the physical is a very important part of the proclamation, the explanation, the learning of the eternal truths, the written word of God, the Bible.

You are a disciple of Jesus

Once you have all this understanding, you can start practicing/training time after time on what you have learned. You are an apprentice, a disciple. As the master does, you do.

What you can give - you have authority over

What you experience freedom and faith to give is your area of authority given by God. Only that which you have revelation comes into the group over which you have authority. As your revelation continues, the area of authority will automatically grow.

This has to do with many years of walking with the Lord. Only those who are willing to walk the path of suffering and pay the price for God's power and be a true Jesus disciple come in here.

What you have authority over is yours

It is a wonderful, experience, knowledge, and feeling to have. Namely, that one has been abandoned by the Lord because of his walk with him. No one can take you away from the areas of authority you have been given. Only you can give them away from you. You can do this by abandoning faith in Christ and walking the path of sin.

"Let us, therefore, pass the children's teaching on Christ and move toward the perfect,… ..

For it is impossible that those who have once been enlightened and have tasted the heavenly gift and have been partakers of the Holy Spirit

And have tasted the good words of God and the powers of the world to come, and then fall away, (Greek Parapipto, falls away in a secure, persuasive way) again can be renewed to repentance, "(Heb. 6, 1-6) Read all the verses.

What I have seen from an incident like this is that he has been hardened. Faith in God, as I could observe, has left him. It was no longer in the person's environment of life, in the person's soul, thoughts or feelings. The person was simply alien from the belief in the living God. He rejected everything.

What is yours - Can you give to whomever you want

This is a wonderful feeling and knowledge. Imagine what grace you can give in freedom that the Lord has given you to whom you will. Anyone you give it to can decide for themselves if they want it. The choices people make are a choice we respect.

Do they want it?

You give it. Then it is God's gift to them through you. The gift of grace is theirs when they receive it, not before.

What you can give to whoever you want - Can be received by anyone who wants it

What you have God's authority to give, you can give to who you are. It is alive in you and through you, to the one you give it to if they want it.

If you give it and it is not received, it may feel closed and difficult for you. However, people are ready to accept the gift of God through you, it feels open and joyful to you.

Anyone who wants it - See it
When I speak in my home country or on the big platforms abroad, the experience is the same. When people in my home country begin to "see" what I speak, when I preach, it becomes completely silent in the hall. This happens every time.
Abroad, the joy, the beat, and the joy break out. We have different sayings on the same thing, but they "see" what I am talking about. It is the revelation of the spoken word that comes to them personally.

6

What do I understand?

"God thundered wonderfully with his voice; he does great things, and we don't understand them. " (Job 37, 5)

There are more negative events happening in the world than ever, but Christians are not. We live in real high prophetic times. That expression is completely worn out, but it now has its relevance like never before.
Wake you up asleep, the Lord will shine for you if you want to be bright and show the way. One said to me: I look on Facebook, there are many Christians there, but all they show are pictures of themselves and their close surroundings. Not too many people show interest in what is happening in society.

40

The Lord wants you to be a warrior of the Spirit

If Christians have never before been interested in society and oriented, then now is the time.

God's will for you is to be a warrior of the Spirit. The Lord wants you to learn how to be. You can only learn this from Him.

If you **understand it, you see it**

If you don't understand it, you won't see it either. We are meant to be the Lord's giants implanted in the world in all arenas. He wants us to influence the whole world by being present spiritual rebirths. So that he can "thunder" through you with his wonderful voice, doing great things around you.

Listen to this. Don't do anything, he'll do it around you because you understand he'll do it around you.

"They understood nothing, and they understand nothing; they walk in darkness; all the foundations of the earth falter. " (Psalm 82: 5)

Politicians and "those who believe they understand themselves and everything"

They have no opportunity for a full understanding of reality. It's all a spiritual battle. All the things we see happening in society now are spiritual attacks from Satan. We who are born again and hear the voice of God must rise and be an echo of the voice of God in us and through us in time in any place. We understand what is happening, the world does not understand it and therefore cannot handle the matter properly.

What is happening on the planet Tellus is all spiritual, there are words and there is spiritual war through the use of words that are all spiritual.

"A senseless man does not know it, and a fool does not understand it." (Psalm 92, 7)

They have no way of understanding, even though it is all up in the day, Satan is blinding their eyes.

"Who will he learn from, and who will understand the message? Are there children who have just weaned from the milk, taken away from the breast? " (Isa 28: 9)

You must take care of your spiritual growth yourself

You must make sure to grow and mature in your Christian life. You may have been born again. That life did not last forever, if not at all times for the right food and the right exercise.
If it does not, you will die spiritually at some point. You fall from faith. That's how it is. Only you can do something about it.

"You shall hear and hear and not understand, see and see and not discern;"

NB! NB!
On the cliff to death in the spirit
These are scary things. Walk around like a dull immature Christian, on the cliff to death in the spirit. You don't understand where it's going. That's just the way it is. It does not help if you think it is good if it is not.

"For this people's hearts are dull, and with their ears, they hear heavy, and their eyes they close, lest they see with their eyes, and hear with their ears, and understand with their heart, and repent, that I may heal them." (Matt 13, 14 - 15)

You give the bark

It's lethal when the lethargy gets hold of you, then you just give the bark. You say: It's going well.

Whenever anyone hears the word about the kingdom and does not understand it, the evil one comes and robs what is sown in his heart; this is what is sown by the road. "

Why could Satan take what was sown in his heart? Yes, because he didn't understand it. This goes two ways. He who preached it did not understand it, then at least the recipient could not understand it. Or simply that the recipient was not interested in it."

Sown in the good soil

But what was sown in the good soil is he who hears the word and understands it; he bears fruit, and one gives a hundred fold, a sixty fold, a thirty fold. " (Matt 13, 19 and 23)

Here we see a different reaction. The word is received, it begins to grow and grow right away. It provides rich fruits and understanding.

"And give your hearts enlightened eyes, that you may understand what hope he has called you to, and how rich in the glory of his inheritance among the saints." (Eph. 1:18)

It is when the understanding, the revelation comes, that things begin to grow. You have begun to understand, you know what you have in Christ, then a powerful spiritual development comes within you.

"Understand what I'm saying! For the Lord will give you understanding of everything. " (2h 2, 7)

NB! NB!
Do you see how important it is that we take hold with the Lord, that we have an intimate fellowship with Him? The Lord will give you a completely personal understanding of everything.

The Word can come to you through a preacher as a revelation in the scriptures or you receive a revelation on God's Word directly yourself. Whichever way it comes, you have to take hold of yourself, believe in patience, and take responsibility for your spiritual life. Then a spiritual growth will start in your life. Not before, don't forget that, you will only fool yourself if you don't do it the right way, Gods way, the Bible way.

7

Sell your faith - don't sell it cheaply, but convincingly

What you believe can make others believe. What you are absolutely convinced of, without a shadow of a doubt, you can make others believe and without a shadow of a doubt as well.

Not a sales trick

These are not "sales techniques, psychological techniques" for selling a product. Many will be able to say you are a sales talent of dimensions. That is not what is the breakthrough effect here. One moves in the world of sensory knowledge, namely the earth. Without knowing that there is another world, a spiritual world. A world without physical matter, a world that cannot be registered by our senses. If we live that way, statements like this will be completely natural. They are blocked from understanding anything else.

The technique of spiritual conviction

"But the fruit of the Spirit of God with the great
Oh, the Holy Spirit is love, joy, peace, longsuf-
fering, gentleness, goodness, faithfulness, meek-
ness, abstinence;" (Gal 5, 22)

"If we live in the Spirit, let us walk in the
Spirit!" (Gal. 5:25)

The beginning of the journey of revelation

When you are willing to do the deeds of the
flesh in your life (Gal. 5, 19 - 21). Please read
these verses. When you are willing to do these
things and you at the same time fill yourself with
God's written words and do in practical action
what the Word of God says. Then you are at the
beginning of the journey to the revelation of the
fruits of the Spirit in your life.
As you emerge from the fruits of the Spirit and
the workings of the flesh, you will experience
revelation in the written Word of God. You will
begin to have a revelation knowledge of it.
When you then prepare to proclaim the gospel,
there are no longer empty theological words, but
they are words of "Spirit and life."

The technique of spiritual conviction

"It is the Spirit that quickeneth, the flesh profiteth nothing; The words that I speak to you are spirit and life. " (John. 6, 63)

NB!
Read my book "Dress up for victory", where I have everything in detail on this topic.

To convince, will cost you everything

Life must be lived in repentance from the deeds of the flesh. There is something uncomfortable for man, but there is no other way to go. If you want to be in the position of a "proclaiming convict"

Get up, sell your faith, expensive and persuasive

Having Christ alive in us costs everything. Being a disciple of Jesus, an apprentice of Jesus will cost you everything. Everything that you have accumulated over the years, through your senses, into your thought and emotional life and further into your flesh, and from there to your surroundings. This must repent, it must all be subject to the authority of Christ. Christ must have control over all of you. It is not difficult to understand that this is a great job that requires will and discipline.

You must build a close relationship with God
Furthermore, the word of God in you and your seeking relationship with God's presence must be done every day. You must establish a close, intimate relationship with God Jehovah. You personally have to get it. You must seek God alone. No one else's can help you, no one else's suggestions can help you here. No books will help you either, God will help you. Little by little, things will move forward. As long as you don't give up, it's a win. Here it is not a matter of how long you will be before God in the silence of prayer. You take all the time it takes, that's the only opportunity for you and everyone else.

Your faith is precious, don't sell it cheap
You are moving forward toward the strongly persuasive belief, which is the strong spiritual belief in you, which is coming through the sanctification in you.

"Paul says, that I may know him (not the knowledge of) and the power of his resurrection, and
the fellowship of his sufferings, being made
equal to him in his death" (Phil. 3:10)

Do you see?
The precious way and go for precious results
if you will?

8

What have I received?

The Divine Truths, we can never say many times to ourselves. Disciple doing is a process where the repetition of the same things is done time and time again until it is stuck. It is just like learning a subject. It is the constant repetition of theory practiced in practice that is ultimately stuck. It is no use folding your hands to pray to God for it to sit, no, here it has to work hard until things are in place.

Think of all the impressions you got through your five senses from when you were a baby until you were saved. This will be done and you will be clothed with the Word of God, which shapes and forms the new life of your soul/personality.

Discipleship is underway as you begin to obey Mark 16, 15. There, the challenges begin in the learning process. So it's just getting started.

Connected to God's power station

When you are connected, all the opportunities on every level of life are ready for you to use in the service of God as the Lord directs you.

Born again and has become a new creature, it is being saved
God had the plan ready for planet earth. First, he created man in his own image and

"God is spirit." (John. 4, 24)

Furthermore, he took

"Earth (Adam) and shaped and formed man (Adam), then he breathed the breath of life into Adam's nose. Adam became a living soul.
" (Genesis 2, 7)

"All things were created by Him, all things in heaven and on earth, the visible and the invisible." (Col 1, 16)

The Bible, God's own Holy Word, guarantees to us that all God Jehovah, the Creator, and Lord of life, is our unlimited and miraculous source of everything we need or want.

The mortal brakes of the curse

God's great plan and dream for us is that we should have more than enough of all that is good. He wants us to enjoy the abundance of all things. It concerns happiness, health, and material goods. The sin put an end to all this almost before it had begun. God's legacy of blessing was abruptly replaced with the legacy of the curse. The degradation of man and the earth was underway.

God's great love for man, made the impossible possible

God immediately set out to look for the key to the lost paradise. He found the key in his own son Jesus Christ. The body of Jesus Christ became the house of God Jehovah himself. This was the only solution to get man back to paradise. God had to give himself as a ransom for the sin of mankind (the inheritance sin) through His Son. When our sins were punished and removed, nothing stood between God and us. When we believe in the good news of what Jesus did on Calvary's cross, God welcomes us back to Himself more.

We are back in God's abundance

"Jesus said, I have come that ye may have life and life in abundance." (Jn 10:10)

It is wonderful, with sin and rebellion out of the way, we can come before God with great boldness. His will is abundance not lacking and distressed. His blessings are here for us now. Jesus came for a purpose, namely to remove the curse and the father and curse of the curse once and for all.

"Jesus came to destroy the works of the devil," (1 John 3, 8)

Including all sin and every evil consequence that weakens and demoralizes society, including material poverty.

You have received this, but let's look at the dangers first
Since this has been so much in focus on material wealth, I would say that it does not involve accumulating wealth,

"And of greed they shall, with fictitious words, exploit you for their gain. But the verdict on them is not old-fashioned, and their forfeiture is not asleep. " (2 Pet. 2, 3)

"Teaches improper teaching for the sake of winning." (Titus 1:11)

"Thus it is with him who gathers treasures and is not rich in God." (Luke. 12, 21)

Material prosperity without God's perspective becomes a seduction of wealth.

Jesus talks about "the seduction of wealth." (Matt. 13:22)

Paul also clearly stated that "love of money is the root of all evil." (1 Tim. 6, 10)

It is not the money itself that is the problem, but it is the love of them.

"Some have gone astray from the belief of desire for this." (1 Tim 6, 10)

Another warning from Jesus comes.

NB! NB!
The necessity of sanctification for victory.

"The worries of this world, the deception of wealth, and the lusts after all else come and suffocate the word so that it will be fruitless." (Mark. 4, 19)

"One day the Lord looked around and said to his disciples, 'How hard it will be for the rich to enter the kingdom of God!' (Mark. 10, 23-24)

"Jesus said, Woe to you, you rich! For you have already received your comfort. " (Luke. 6, 24)

This can happen if you are not careful. The material can take over completely. I include the verse from Luke again.

"Thus it is with him who gathers treasures and is not rich in God." (Luke. 12, 21)

Paul warned the Apostle Timothy and the Christians of Ephesus, Listen to what the Bible says:

"But those who want to become rich fall into temptation and snare and many bad and harmful desires, which lower people into ruin and perdition.

For the love of money is a root of all evil; of desire for this, some have gone astray from the faith and have pierced themselves with many pains.

Invite those who are rich in this present world, not to be overbearing or to hope for the uncertain riches, but to God who gives us abundantly all things to enjoy," (1 Tim. 6: 9-17).

Here again, you see the importance of a balanced relationship in your life with God, the traps are waiting for you. Then build up your strength in the Lord.

prosperity Phobia

The traditional Christian teaching has placed such great emphasis on these warnings. Believers have seen poverty as spirituality. They have seen prosperity as wickedness.

In the preaching of faith that has passed the world over the last 40 years, being "blessed" with wealth has been a pretty big point. This, over time, has created a prosperity phobia that hinders the advancement and growth of the gospel. Don't let the money become your idol. Yes, we Christians are part of God's royal family. We experience ourselves upstairs, we live in victory in all that is good. The Lord's blessing is upon us. We are chosen and shown the trust of our Lord. Don't fall into my dear friend and build a castle for yourself.

Financial blessing for a purpose
We must live in a financially rich blessing for one reason. Our money is meant to be used to get the gospel out to those whom the Lord has asked us to give it to in the mission command. Read Mark 16, 15, Matt 28, 18 - 20, Matt 24, 14 and Rev 5, 9.

Prosperity for a purpose, giving money so that the gospel of all creation can be completed as soon as possible for Jesus to come again

"After the gospel of the glory of the Blessed
God, that which is entrusted to me."
(1 Tim. 1:11)

"But just as we are honored by God for the
gospel being entrusted to us, so we speak, not as
those who want to be human, but as God who
tries our hearts." (1 Thess. 24)

We have been entrusted with giving the gospel to
all people in the world.

"Jesus said to the disciples: Therefore, go out
into all the world and preach the gospel to all
creation." (Mark. 16, 15)

It takes money to get this job done. That is why
the Lord alone wants His children to have material prosperity, just as their soul and spirit have
spiritual prosperity.

"You loved! I want you in all parts to feel good
and be in good health, just like your soul is well.
" (3 John. 2)

Balanced understanding

With a balanced understanding of what the Bible says about material prosperity, the following statements will nurture your beliefs and encourage it to expect material prosperity as a believer, who has a heart that is purposeful in conveying the good news to the unconverted.

"Fear the Lord your saints. For those who fear Him, there is no shortage. " (Psalm 34:10)

"My God will fill all their cravings." (Phil. 4: 9)

"I want you to feel good in every way."
(3 John. 2)

This applies to general wealth and includes material wealth.

"For the Lord is pleased that His servants are well." (Psalm 35, 27)

"The Lord will give you more than enough of all that is good in goods, by your fruit of life, by what your livestock carries, and by the crop of your soil." (Deut. 28:11)

"For the Lord shall open his good treasury."
(Deut. 28:12)

"It is the Lord's blessing that makes
rich." (Proverbs 10, 22)

"The Lord will command the blessing to come
upon you and reach you in everything you put
your hands to do." (Deut. 28: 8)

A condition for the fulfillment of this.

The condition is that you believe it.

"Don't fear, just believe." (Mark. 5, 36)

"Without faith, it is impossible" (Heb. 11, 6)

Faith in all the gospel truths must be in place.
And that you are set free from your sins, with
everything else it entails.

"Christ redeemed us from the curse of the law,
being a curse to us - for it is written, cursed is
every one that hangeth on a tree -" (Gal. 3:13).

Material poverty is part of the curse

It is salvation, salvation, it is liberation from Satan's authority and influence over our lives. It is freedom from the judgment of death upon us, from the plagues of disease, from material deficiency, and all the works of the devil.

"For this, the Son of God is manifest that he will put an end to the works of the devil."
(1 John. 3: 8)

I have been preaching this message to the world since I was a young man. That is what Christ affirms

"But they went out and preached the word everywhere, and the Lord acted and confirmed the word by the signs that came." (Mark. 16, 20)

This is the message that works – The circle of love

When everything is in its right place. Now it's your turn, it works for you too.

Bible verses that build your faith for what God wants you to receive

These are verses that you plant in your spirit through the study of them. This will bring abundance in your life and through your life to the world around you. You receive to pass on, it is always circulating

"The circle of love of all that is good"

"Give glory to the Lord with what you own and the first fruits of all your crops! Then your storehouses will be filled to abundance, and your wine vessels will overflow with most"
(Proverbs 3, 9-10)

God challenges you to bring your money to Him and try Him to see if the blessing comes your way

"See if he will not open the windows of heaven, and pour out blessings upon you, so much so that there will not be enough room to receive it."
(Mal. 3, 10)

"For the Lord God saith, Flour shall not be empty, neither shall the oil-vessel be dry."

64

(1 Kings 17:14)

"For the earth is the Lord's and what fills it." 1 Cor. 10, 26)

"Wealth and prosperity are the gifts of the Lord." (Ecclesiastes 5, 19)

"Then you shall have happiness on your paths." (Joshua 1: 8)

"But seek first the kingdom of God and His righteousness, and all things will be forgiven!" (Matt. 6:33)

"The Lord is your shepherd; you shall not lack anything." (Psalm 23, 1)

"He will keep no good from those who walk in righteousness." (Psalm 84:11)

"Blessed is every one that feareth the Lord, that delighteth in his commandments ... and riches shall be in his house." (Psalm 112, 1.3)

"You shall remember the Lord your God: for it is He who gives you the ability to gain prosperity." (Deut. 8:18)

"The silver and the gold are mine," says the Lord. (Hag. 2, 8)

"The whole earth is mine." (Ex. 19: 5)

"Every animal in the forest is mine, and the animals of a thousand heights are mine." (Psalm 50, 10)

"Oh, how precious your mercy is, God. Therefore, the children of men… have taken refuge… in the shadow of your wings. They are saturated abundantly by the abundance of your house ... because with you is the source of life. " (Psalm 36, 7 - 9)

"The blessing of the Lord maketh rich, his own endeavor adds nothing" (Proverbs 10, 22)

"O Lord, how many are your deeds ... You did them all wisely; the earth opening is of what you have created.

"You give them, they sink; you open your hand, they saturate well. " (Psalm 104, 24, 28)

"I love those who love me, and those who seek me will find me.

With me is wealth and honor, old inheritance, and justice.

"Therefore, I give those who love me true wealth to inheritance and fill their storehouses." (Proverbs 8, 17 - 18 and 21)10)

"Blessed art thou, Lord God ... For all that is in heaven is yours: both honor and riches come from thee." (1 Chronicles 29, 10 - 12)

"Walk in the ways of God ... so you can do well in everything you set out to do and wherever you went." (1 Kings 2, 3)

"Praised be the Lord, who daily blesses us with goods." (Psalm 68, 19)

"A faithful man receives rich blessings." (Proverbs 28:20)

"Jesus said, I have come that you may have life and life in abundance." (John 10:10)

Here you see evidence in abundance
Everything material that you can see around you is a product of the Lord. This is a strong affirmation that the Lord's will for man to be well material, as well as physically and spiritually blessed.

The Bible says so clearly: "No one has left a house or brothers or sisters or father or wife or children or fields for my sake or for the sake of the gospel, who will not have a hundredfold left in time, house and family and fields… and in the world to come, eternal life. " (Mark 10, 29-30) |

"The circle of love of all that is good"

9

NB! NB!
Be more than convinced
of what you believe

"Faith is full wisdom of what is hoped for, conviction of things not seen." (Heb. 11: 1)

Stretch your belief until you have it as a solid rock of faith established
This is the very strength of faith you receive as you stretch towards it. Don't give up until you have it. This I explain carefully in other of my books.

"By faith we understand that the world is made by the word of God, so that what is seen was not made manifest." (Heb. 11, 3)

This is what you accept and know is the way things happen. God himself gave us the first and best example of this, already in Genesis 1, 3-4.

"Then God said: It will be light! And it became light,

And God saw that the light was good, and God separated the light from the darkness. "
(Genesis 1, 3 - 4)

Do you see
"God spoke and it happened, he commanded and it stood there." (Psalm 33: 9)

Be rock solid to your point of view here. This is what matters, nothing else
"But without faith, it is impossible to please God; for he who comes before God must believe that he exists, and that he pays to him who seeks Him." (Heb 11, 6)

Believe the setting baked into you
The attitude of positive strong faith must be baked into you, so that you will no doubt go against the answers of God. Listen to this:

"By faith, Sarah also had the power to establish a family, and that despite her age, when she faithfully considered Him who gave the promise. Do you see how the attitude, attitude and behavior of the faith was baked into them.

The same way and stronger

In the same way and stronger, it will be in you and me under the new covenant. We are the soldiers of Christ, we are the "disciples of the Lord".

The victory is ours, if we believe it.

With this belief baked in, you are the proclaimer / poet of your time

"Therefore, let us, when we have so great a cloud of witnesses around us, put away all that is burdensome, and the sin that so clings to us, and run with patience in the battle which is ours,

As we look at the originator and consummate of the faith, Jesus Christ, the one who, for the joy that awaited Him, patiently led the cross, without regard for dishonor, and now sits on the right side of God's throne. " (Heb 12, 1-2)

"It is for the sake of discipline that you endure suffering; (Heb 12, 7)

Believe the giants never give up
The seed sown in you grows in good soil. The good earth is you when you do / believe the word of the Lord. You put it into practice. You set it out to do what the word says.

You have a whole new life style, a whole new way of thinking, a new language.
You pass on these new Divine qualities in your life. Let all the truths of God become a solid understanding in your mind. It then becomes what you live out in practice.

Your character becomes a character of faith
My whole life as a born-again Christian is built on studying scripture and acting on God's promises, time after time, year after year, ten years after ten years. Reality, conviction grows firmly in you, in your soul and in your spirit.

"Is not my word like a fire, saith the Lord, and like a hammer that breaketh the rock?"
(Jer. 23, 29)

"The sword of the Spirit, which is the word of God" (Eph. 6:17)Do you see how the attitude, attitude and behavior of the faith were baked into them? In the same way and stronger, it will be in you and me under the new covenant. We are the soldiers of Christ, we are the "disciples of the Lord".
The victory is ours if we believe it.

With this belief baked in, you are the proclaimer/poet of your time

"Therefore, let us, when we have so great a cloud of witnesses around us, put away all that is burdensome, and the sin that so clings to us, and run with patience in the battle which is ours,

As we look at the originator and consummate of the faith, Jesus Christ, the one who, for the joy that awaited Him, patiently led the cross, without regard for dishonor, and now sits on the right side of God's throne. " (Heb 12, 1-2)

"It is for the sake of discipline that you endure suffering; (Heb 12, 7)

Believe the giants never give up

The seed sown in you grows in good soil. The good earth is you when you do/believe the word of the Lord. You put it into practice. You set it out to do what the word says.

You have a whole new lifestyle, a whole new way of thinking, a new language.
You pass on these new Divine qualities in your life. Let all the truths of God become a solid understanding of your mind. It then becomes what you live out in practice.

Your character becomes a character of faith – if you pay the gigantic price

My whole life as a born-again Christian is built on studying scripture and acting on God's promises, time after time, year after year, ten years after ten years. The reality, the conviction grows firmly in you, in your soul, and in your spirit.

"Is not my word like a fire, saith the Lord, and like a hammer that breaketh the rock?"
(Jer. 23, 29)

"The sword of the Spirit, which is the word of God" (Eph. 6:17)

We enter the enemy territory with knowledge of who we are in Christ

We oppose any seductive tactics that Satan is trying, which seems destructive, or that go against the truths of salvation.

In this way we fight the good fight of faith, this is spiritual warfare. This and nothing else. The word of God has eternal victory through your mouth.

We enter Satan's camp with the proclamation of the gospel with strength is spiritual warfare

We transmit the gospel message of Jesus Christ with faith and strength to individuals or crowds, then we fight against powers and authorities, against the spirit armies of evil.

In every place where the gospel is believed, Satan's fortifications are torn down in people's lives. Prisoners are set free from the power of darkness and put into the kingdom of our God.

"He who delivered us out of the power of darkness, and put us into the kingdom of his beloved Son," (Col. 1:13)

This is the task of the reborn individual and community. This is the mission of the Christians in their entirety.

"But thank God, who gives us the victory through our Lord Jesus Christ!" (1 Cor. 15, 57)

"For this is the victory that has overcome the world, our faith." (1 John. 5, 4)

"As we know the fear of the Lord, we seek to win people." (2 Cor. 5: 11)

We win people for Christ through the proclamation of the gospel truths, through spiritual warfare, through the good fight of faith.

The victorious spiritual warfare
There are Christians who believe they are fighting for authority against government, and the spirit armies of evil in heaven - in the congregation, in the community, in the body of Jesus. Be-

lievers who are going to drive out evil spirits from other Christians.

This perspective on "spiritual warfare" does not have its basis in scripture, but conflicts with the gospel and shows a lack of understanding of the truths concerning salvation.

This is because one does not live up to what the scriptures are asking us to do, one lives in dis-obedience to the word.

The power of faith

Then one does not gain the spiritual experiences of faith and is not guided through the trials nec-essary for spiritual growth, through the revela-tion of the spirit, which in turn gives rise to the growth and power of faith. Which in turn makes you a stronger and stronger proclaimer of the gospel of Jesus Christ the living Son of God.

Be more than convinced of what you believe

Then those you speak to will be convinced too. They will seize the beginning of strong faith in their lives there and then. They will be at the start line, and continue from there, if they want.

Proclaim the gospel of peace with all your senses to the senses of all people in the Holy Spirit.

1 0

You are God's voice to the world

"And the Lord will guide you at all times and saturate you in the midst of the wilderness; (Jes. 54:11)

"Jesus said: Those who believe in me as the scripture has said, out of his life shall flow streams of living water.

This he said of the Spirit that they should receive who believed in him, for the Spirit had not yet come, because Jesus was not yet glorified. " (John 7, 38-39)

The day came and the Spirit fell (Pentecost Day, Acts 1 and 2, Joel 3)
Can you see it? The Spirit of God materialized in you, the Spirit of God through you as the invert-er.

You have to believe it conscious first

You are God's voice to the world, believe it, then those who hear you will believe it too. Your faith in what you do releases the power of the Holy Spirit through you to those around you.

From spirit to physical substance through you

From being spiritual thoughts that come to you and becoming the realities of sensory knowledge through you, this must happen.

You have to believe the thoughts that have come to you

The moment you believe the thoughts of the Word of God that have come to you, and act on those in faith, Living Gods' thoughts are made into physical practice.

Then comes the physical reality of what you believe.

"How beautiful on the mountains are their feet that come with glad tidings, who proclaim peace, who carry good news, who proclaim salvation." (Isa. 52: 7)

You are the voice

You are the voice of God, you are the messenger, you are the voice and words of Christ. Believe it, act on it and you will see the result of it. This is the struggle in spirit.

"Since His Divine power has given us everything that serves life and Godly fear, through the knowledge of Him who calls us by His own glory and power.

And thereby have given us the greatest and most precious promises, that by them ye may be partakers of the Divine nature… "(2 Peter 1, 3 - 4)

To the extent that Christ is in you - you will be his mouth

This is important to understand, with the conviction of faith. When you do, you have it. It's a long way to go to get it all "steeled" in you. This is the process of sanctification that must go its way. The laying down of the works of the flesh and the dressing of the fruits of the Spirit.
(Gal. 5)

This comes little by little in obedience to the written Word of God. Here your willed life must put everything.

God's nature is "Eternal Life"

"Jesus said, The devil comes only to steal, murder, and destroy, but I have come that you may have life and life in abundance." (John 10:10)

"By faith, we understand that the world is made by the word of God so that what is seen was not made manifest." (Heb. 11, 3)

Bring this to you: "As we have not the visible to the eye, but the invisible; for the visible is temporal, but the invisible is eternal. " (2 Cor. 4: 18)

Do you see that? The strength of faith brings the results

The nature that more and more takes over in your life by the nature of sin is the nature called "eternal life". This is God's own eternal life. God's divine revelations come to you, more and more as the flesh is laid down and the fruits of the Spirit take over the place of your life.

The revelations of God give the full certainty

It is the revelations of God that give you the full certainty, which is the "steel" faith. Said in a slightly joking word. It is God himself who comes with the revelations.

"Faith is full certainty of what is hoped for, conviction of things that are not ness." (Heb. 11: 1)

Here you have it.

This life is God Himself.

He is the creator of all things, the whole cosmos and everything behind the cosmos, the eternity of eternity. This is manifested in creation and given to us in Christ Jesus.

Everything in Him is given to us in the new creation

Can you discern the size of what you are in Christ Jesus?

We have it - the Gentiles have not

They can get it through you and me. Believe it and do it - then the Gentiles will believe it too.

Wherever you go to a Gentile nation and proclaim the message of Jesus that you believe - then they will believe it too.

Try it out, buy a plane ticket and travel. Proclaim the challenging gospel that you believe in and the results will not fail.

Do you see the importance?
Do you mean to go with God, then you must. God wants you as His voice to the world, through His Son Jesus Christ through the Holy Spirit within you.

What you have in Christ you can give when you believe it.

The world dies if we don't give it life. I'm not talking about religious rallies and worship.

They will believe or reject what you proclaim
I'm talking about the challenging proclamation of Jesus Christ in strong conscious faith in Him. Then those you speak to will believe what you proclaim or reject it. That case is perfectly fine. Everything is a free choice, but we give them the opportunity to receive the resurrected Jesus Christ, as their savior and rebirth. They have the

opportunity to become a new creation in Jesus Christ. This is absolutely amazing. This is the God given the opportunity for eternal life in glory. People get the opportunity for a whole new start, a whole new life.

Listen to this:
"For the word of the cross is folly to him that perisheth, but to us that are saved, it is the power of God;" (1 Cor. 1:18)

Are you ready for the glory to work through you?
You are God's miracle human on earth today.
You can give the world the miracle it needs now.
It is in your spirit everything. You can let it flow out of your mouth.
Let your voice help people. You don't stand up to people with something you "hope" works.

The life of God is in you, you are the life of God and you know it, you believe it. It works through you. The glory is in you.

As Jesus said he was from God, you can say: I am from God.

"When John the Baptist was in prison, he sent
his disciples to Jesus: Are you the one to come,
or will we wait for another?

And Jesus answered and said, go away, tell John
what ye hear and see:

The blind see and the lame walk, the lepers are
cleansed and the deaf hear and the dead rise and
the gospel is preached to the poor;
(Matt. 11, 3-5)

This is the evidence in the physical world
Believe it, proclaim it, prove it in Jesus name.
Make the people believe it.
You can say: I'm a conqueror
One who overcomes everything in the name of
Jesus.

"You are of God my children (we who are born
again) and have overcome them, for he who is in
you is greater than he who is in the world."
(1 John. 4,4)

"For all that is born of God overcomes the world, and this is the victory that has overcome the world, our faith." (1 John. 5, 4)

Do you see the fierce victory in us born again?
Faith is the key that makes the Gentiles believe the gospel
You have the key. You can make the Gentiles believe the message you are proclaiming.

You were born to victory
The secret to "living" and "being" in the word, the word of the Bible, is that you stand before the world, for the heathen that one overcomes with the word on your lips. You stand out as God's overcoming son in Jesus Christ.

"For though we walk in the flesh, we do not fight in a carnal way;

For our weapons of war are not carnal, but mighty for God to overthrow fortifications; As we overthrow thought-buildings and every height that rises against the knowledge of God, and capture every thought under obedience to Christ, the word of God "(Ways translation)."

87

(2 Cor. 10: 3-5)

This has surprised many

This has surprised many, they have not seen it, they have not looked for it. They have not appreciated what they have in Christ. The Bible will speak to you all you are in Christ Jesus. Let the Bible guide your life. Let God's Word, the Bible, lead your life to victory in all areas.
Let other people's lives be led to victory by the Word of God working through you to them.

This is how the war is won every time

Are you born again, baptized in the Holy Spirit and filled with the Word of God? Then you are filled with the life of the Spirit of God who can help people, just in whatever spiritual words you are filled with. You believe the words and proclaim them. People see you think they, then they believe it too and accept and get their needs met.

"The word is near you, in your mouth and in your heart (spirit) that is the word of faith, that which we preach." (Rom. 10: 8)

"By the way - be strong in the Lord and in the
power of His might!

Put on the full armor of God so that you can
stand against the devil's cunning attack;

For we have no fight against flesh and blood, but
against powers, against the authorities, against
the lords of the world in this darkness, against
the spirit of evil - armies in the heavenly, the
spirit atmosphere in Cosmos.
Therefore, put on the full armor of God so that
you can resist the evil day and stand after overcoming everything.

Then stand girded about their loins with truth,
and clothed with the armor of righteousness,

And bound on their feet with the skill of battle
that the gospel of peace provides,

And grasp besides all this shield of faith, with
which you can extinguish all the burning arrows
of evil,

And take the helmet of salvation and the sword
of the Spirit, which is the word of God,

As you pray in the Spirit at all times with all
prayer and invocation and are vigilant therein
with all endurance and prayer for all the saints,

And also for me, that I must give words when I
open my mouth, that I may boldly announce the
secret of the gospel, "(Eph. 6, 10-19).

"And they have triumphed over him by the blood
of the lamb and the words which they
testified." (Rev. 12, 10)

"He disarmed the powers and authorities and
openly questioned them, appearing to be victorious over them on the cross." (Co.1 2, 15)

"The Lord says, Behold, I will make my words
in your mouth a fire." (Jer. 5,14)

"But Him, the Word, which can do more than
anything, far beyond what we pray or understand, by the power that works in us."
(Eph. 3:20)

"And behold, I am with you all the days until the end of the world." (Matt. 28:20)

What superior victory, what more than a victorious victory, the eternal victory. This victory is given to you to believe and proclaim, so that faith is spread and activated in every place you come.

11

God's miracle gift to the world

The gift God gave

"For God so loved the world that He gave His own Son, the only-begotten, that whoever believes in Him should not perish but have eternal life." (John. 3:16)

"In the beginning was the Word and the Word was with God, and the Word was God."
(John. 1, 1)

"They came near to the gates of death.

Then they cried out to the Lord in their distress, and out of their afflictions, he saved them.

He sent his word and healed them and saved them from their graves." (Psalm 107, 18-20)

"And the Word became flesh and dwelt among us, and we saw his glory - a glory which the only begotten Son hath of his Father full of grace and truth." (John. 1:14)

Jesus' miracle birth

"And the angel said unto her, Fear not, Mary" for thou hast found grace with God;

And behold, thou shalt conceive and bear a son, and shalt call his name Jesus.

He shall be great and shall be called the Son of the Highest, and the Lord God will give him the throne of David his father,

And he shall reign over the house of Jacob forever, and his kingdom shall not end.

But Mary said to the angel: How is this going to happen, as I do not know of man)

And the angel answered her, The Holy Spirit shall come upon thee, and the power of the Highest shall overshadow thee; therefore, also the holy one who is born shall be called the Son of God. "(Luke. 1, 30, 35)

"For the soul (personality) of the flesh is in the blood." (Deut. 17:11)

Let's see how this happened.

The second Adam - Christ Jesus came to earth

"Therefore, as he enters the world, he says: You would not have sacrifices and gifts, but a body you formed for me." (Heb. 10, 5)

"He who, when he was in the form of God, did not regard it as a prey to be like God,

But of course, he renounced it and took on the form of a servant, coming in the likeness of men. " (Philip. 2: 6-7)

Jesus said to them, Verily, verily, I say unto you, Before Abraham came into being, I am.

Then they took up stones to throw at him, but Jesus hid himself and went out of the temple. " (John. 8, 58-59)

God came in His Son to the salvation of mankind

"He came to his own, and his own did not receive him." (John. 3,11)

"But all who received him gave him the right to become children of God, those who believe in his name;" (John. 1:12)

You made a body for me

"You made a body for me." (Heb. 10, 5)

A body made/created in heaven, in the same building material that we are formed in on planet earth. That body was made perfect and breathed with soul and spirit, up into heaven, and then transported to earth. There the Virgin Mary was overshadowed by the Holy Spirit.

Jesus the Son of God, the second Adam

The perfect body, the other Adam was placed in the Virgin Mary's womb. There, the child named Jesus developed for his birthday. The child was sealed behind the virgin for the birthday. Then the hymen was broken from the inside. This was the first and last time in human history this happened.

Fully God and fully human

God himself came down to earth, in the form of his son. God's own Spirit was in Christ, it was the Holy Spirit, that was fully God in Christ. The personality/soul of Jesus had, was the personality of the Son of God. It was the life of Jesus as a human being.

Everything that happened on earth, Jesus had to decide for himself. He knew that he had come to earth to redeem humanity from their sins and bring them back in fellowship with God Jehovah. Jesus had to do this task of his own free will., if it were to have the redeeming effect that could bring man back to God.

"Jesus / He came for us to have life and life in abundance." (John. 10:10)

The second Adam came to earth for a purpose

Christ the second Adam came to earth for a purpose.

To conquer Satan

"For this the Son of God is revealed to end the works of the devil." (1 John. 3: 8)

Satan was the only one who knew that God walked among us in his Son. The other Adam had come. Satan showed his days were counted. God won a perfect victory for all eternity over Satan and the demons, yes over the power of sin.

"You also who were dead by your transgressions and the foreskin of your flesh, you have made him alive with Christ, forgiving us all our sins,

And obliterated the guilt letter, which was written with a commandment, he took it away as he nailed it to the cross.

He disarmed the powers and authorities and openly questioned them, appearing to be victorious over them, Satan and the demons, on the cross. " (Col. 2, 13-15)

The eternal victory was won. Jesus has traveled back to His Father in heaven. At the same time Jesus is here in us who are born again and are filled with the power of the Holy Spirit.

Imagine which Divine journey
You believe the Word and proclaim it - those you proclaim it to will also believe it. You see, our victory is our faith and new life as a born again believer in Christ

It was no wonder the devil hated Jesus Christ
Jesus was God Jehovah, the self-existent who reveals himself and is eternal.
God the creator of the cosmos and everything outside there, wandered around this micro planet for thirty-three and a half years. The only one knew who he was, it was the devil. Mankind had no idea.

"Jesus said to them, Verily, verily, I say unto you, Before Abraham came into being, I am.

Then they took up stones to throw at Him, but Jesus hid and went out of the temple. "

98

(John. 8, 58-59)

Jesus had come very close to telling who he really was -
People in the world of sensory knowledge were unable to understand the spiritual perspective.

"But of the resurrection of the dead, then ye have not read what ye have been told of God, saying,

I am Abraham, Isaac and Jacob the God? Neither is the God of the dead, but the living. "
(Matt. 22 31 - 32)

This was the limit to what the Lord could reveal
We who are believers can look back on this and recognize this as God of the Old Testament.
This is because of the revelation knowledge in Paul's letter.

We read, "I who was circumcised on the eighth day, of the seed of Israel, of the tribe of Benjamin, a Hebrew of Hebrews, before the law a Pharisee,

In zeal a persecutor of the congregation, in righteousness according to the law immaculate.

But what was my gain, for Christ's sake, I have forfeited;
Yes, I value and indeed all loss, because the knowledge of Christ Jesus, my Lord, is so much more valuable, for whose sake I have suffered loss of everything, and I consider it too scarce for me to win Christ

And be in Him, not with my righteousness, who is of the law, but with him who is obtained through faith in Christ, the righteousness of God because of faith, "(Phil. 2: 5 - 9).

This is Jesus' earthly miracle walk
"And as everyone must confess, as the secret of the fear of God: He who was revealed in flesh, justified (took his right) in spirit, seen by angels, preached among peoples, believed in the world, occupied in glory." (1 Tim. 3, 16)

The saddest hike ever to have walked the earth

God's earthly walk was the saddest walk ever to take place on earth. Jesus did not come down to earth to have a joyful life, Jesus came here to earth for a very special purpose, a purpose he knew all about, a purpose necessary for the salvation of mankind.

God himself walked around in the shape of a man

A journey of suffering through a life of thirty-three and a half years. It is impossible for a human being to understand what this meant. It was God Himself walking around in the shape of a man, in the body of his son Jesus.

"Pilate saith unto them, what then shall I do unto Jesus, which they call the Messiah? They all say: Let him crucify!

He then said: What evil then has he done? But they cried even louder: Let him crucify"

And when Pilate saw that there was nothing done, but that there was but a great tumult, he took water, and washed his hands before the eyes of the people, and said, I am innocent in the blood of this righteous man; see you there!

And all the people answered and said, His blood be upon us and upon our children.

Then he released Barabbas, but Jesus they whipped of his skin and surrendered him to be crucified. " (Matt. 27, 22 - 26)

God's own covenant people cried: let him crucify. What a tragedy, but what a victory. Can you see it? All the victories of God are born through the path of suffering. As it was with Christ Jesus, so will it be with us. He walked the path of suffering and won an eternal redemption for humanity.
We walk our path of suffering and are prepared to bring the victory of Jesus' redemption to humanity worldwide.

Listen to this Bible site: "He who knew none of the lords of this world, for had they known him, they would not have crucified the Lord of glory." (1 Cor. 2: 8)

Jesus' miracle of death and resurrection

"He who gave himself up for our sins, to deliver us out of the present evil world according to the will of our God Father." (Gal. 1, 4)

"And when he was found as a man, he humbled himself, so that he became obedient unto death, even the death of the cross." (Phil 2: 8)

No one could take Jesus' life, He gave his life No one could take Jesus' life. He was Lord of death and grave. He volunteered his life for the redemption and salvation of all mankind. Mankind's redemption from the curse into God's rich blessing and love,

Our Savior Jesus' victorious suffering story
"He was despised and forsaken by men, a man full of torment and well acquainted with sick ness; he was as one whom people hide his face from, despised, and we disregarded him for nothing.

Verily, our diseases he hath taken, and our pains he hath borne; but we esteemed him to be afflicted, beaten by God, and made miserable.

But he is wounded for our transgressions, broken for our iniquities; the punishment lay upon him, that we might have peace, and by his wounds, we have been healed.

We, for every wild thing that gets, we each turned to their own ways; but the Lord caused his iniquities to befall him. He was abused even when he was miserable, and he did not open his mouth, like a lamb carried away for slaughter, and like a sheep that keep silent as they cut it; he did not open his mouth.

By tribulation and judgment, he was taken away; but who in his day thought that when he was exterminated by the land of the living, it was for the iniquity of my people that the plague struck him?

They gave him his grave among the wicked, but with a rich man, he was in his death, because he had done no wrong, and there was no betrayal in his mouth.

But it pleased the Lord to crush him; he struck him with sickness; when his soul offered the guilt offering, he should see the offspring and live long, and the will of the Lord should prosper at his hand. " (Jes. 53, 3-10)

Do you see what he gave to us all?
"When Jesus had received the vinegar, he said, It is finished, and he bowed his head and gave up his spirit." (John. 19, 30)

The moment the victory was won and Jesus said "It is finished," the tombs opened in the area of the crucifixion and the dead went out and appeared to many.

The curtain cracked and the tombs opened
"And behold, the curtain of the temple was broken in two pieces from top to bottom, and the earth trembled, and the rocks were broken;

And the tombs were opened, and many bodies of the sleeping saints stood up,

And they went out of the tombs after his resurrection, and came into the holy city, and appeared unto many.

But when the centurion and those who were watching over Jesus saw the earthquake and what was happening, they were horrified and said,

"Truly, this was the Son of God."
(Matt. 27, 51-54)

Can you see what message we have to proclaim in the power of the Spirit to the part of humanity that has not yet heard the gospel? That is what Jesus needs to come again.

You!!
Take these verses you who is the proclaimer, the poet, the maker of evidence (the martyr), the disciple of Jesus, as your very personal command, the very personal task of God. Go with it with courage and boldness as you have never done.

"Jesus said to the disciples, Go out into the world and make all nations my disciples." (Mark 16, 15)

"And Jesus came and spake unto them, saying, All power is given unto me in heaven and on earth;

Therefore go out and make all nations a disciple, baptizing them in the name of the Father, of the Son, and of the Holy Spirit,

And teach them to keep what I have commanded you. And behold, I am with you all the days until the end of the world. " (Matt. 28, 18-20)

"Jesus said, And this gospel of the kingdom shall be preached throughout the world to a testimony (martyrdom) of all peoples, and then shall the end come." (Matt. 24:14)

"Because you were slaughtered and with your blood bought to God from every tribe and tongue and people and offspring," (Rev. 5, 9)

"Time to harvest has come; for harvesting on earth is overpowering. " (Rev 14, 15)

1 2

Miracles are for the world

"Paul said: My speech and preaching were not words of wisdom (sense knowledge), but of the evidence of Spirit and power.

So that their faith should not be based on human wisdom (sensory knowledge) but on the power of God. " (1 Cor. 2, 4 - 5)

Why Evidence of Spirit and Power to the Corinthian Community (koinonia)?
It was God's divine, supernatural, spiritual power, beyond the physical possibility, that was to be the evidence of God's presence and his redeeming power in his son Jesus Christ. Paul understood this and lived in the dimension of his life that you can too.

Spirit proof

This proof is the proof of God's character in you, the proof of his existence in you. Listen:

"God is spirit" (John. 4, 24)

"God is love" (John. 4, 16)

The evidence of the Spirit is the love of Jesus revealed through your personality to the world around you. This is the human experience of Christ in you. This is amazing, to the extent that Christ is in you with strength, the demons and Satan's world in spirit will respond to you as well.
After you have experienced Christ through a human being, you know it is true.
It is the feeling and the visual of the person the people experience, in conjunction with the revelation that is preached. To say it with revelation in an easy-to-understand way is the easy way to understand and believe what is being proclaimed, poetically.

Proof of power

Read carefully what the coming verses explain to you.

"Jesus said to the disciples: and as you depart, preach the kingdom of heaven is at hand!

heal the sick, raise the dead, cleanse leprosy, cast out evil spirits, for nothing has you received, for nothing will you give it. " (Matt. 10, 7-8)

"Jesus answered and said unto them, An evil and unfaithful generation requires signs, and signs shall not be given it, except the sign of the prophet Jonah.

For as Jonas was three days and three nights in the belly of the fish, so shall the Son of man be three days and three nights in the bosom of the earth." (Matt. 12, 39-40)

"Then Jesus began to rebuke the cities where most of his mighty works were done because they had not repented;

Woe to you, Korasin! Woe to you, Bethsaida! If the mighty works that were done in you were done in Tire and Sidon, then they would have long ago converted to sackcloth and ashes.

However, I say to you, it will be more tolerable for Tire and Sidon in the day of judgment than you.

And you Capernaum, who has been exalted to heaven! Just to the realm of death, you will be supported; for if the mighty works which were done in you were done in Sodom, it would stand unto this day. " Matt. 11, 20 - 23)

There is no longer any excuse

When it comes to the power of evidence, we see the seriousness of having experienced the power of God. There is no longer any excuse for not being born again, yes, being saved. You know with full conviction that this is the truth and the saving of your life.

The choice is yours

If you choose no, then it is your free choice that must be respected. But at the end of your life,

what happen then, I don't know. What I can do
is give you the opportunity to meet Christ
through the power of demonstrations of God's
glory now.

What is the proof of power?

**The last thing Jesus said to his disciples be-
fore he was lifted up to heaven in Acts 1, 9
was:**
"But ye shall have power in the coming of the
Holy Ghost, and ye shall be my witnesses (martyrs, proof-makers), both in Jerusalem, and
throughout Judea and Samaria, and even unto
the ends of the earth." (Acts 1: 8)

What Jesus said here between verses 8 and 9, we
can see in Mark 16, 15 - 20, where he said:

"Go out into the world and preach the gospel to
all creation.

And these signs shall follow him that believeth,
in my name shall they cast out devils, they shall
speak with tongues;

They will take snakes in their hands, and if they drink something poisonous it will not harm them; on sick, they will lay their hands and they shall be healed.

Then, after speaking to them, the Lord Jesus was taken to heaven and sat down at God's right hand.

But they went out and preached the word everywhere, and the Lord helped confirm the word by the signs that came with it. " (Mark. 16, 15-20)

Christ knew what was needed
It was compelling miracles for the physical world, a demonstration of the spiritual reality that was needed and it started with the disciples of Jesus and continues to this day.

It's always the same experience
I always find in meetings around the world that miracles of all variants and demons come out, without having done anything. If we have the right understanding, revelation, willingness, faith, and surrender, God will flow through us with the power of His Holy Spirit.

We are first and foremost a witness of Jesus Christ

Paul tells us that Jesus appeared to him and called him to service.

"Therefore, I revealed myself to you, to make you a servant and a witness." (Acts. 1, 21-22)

Let's hear what the disciples said:

"Therefore, one of those who walked with us in all the time the Lord Jesus went in and out of us, right from his baptism at John until the day he was taken from us - one of them should be a witness with us about his resurrection. " (Acts 1, 21-22)

Here it was not important for him to be an apostle, but first and foremost a witness. It is the witness who convinces. The witness has seen, the witness has learned and the witness can, with credibility, pass on affirmations of the divine truths.

Many will say: I don't have enough faith - God's Word says: you have enough faith

"All that is born of God overcomes the world, and this is the victory that overcometh the world, our faith." (1 John. 5, 4)

Many will say: I don't have enough power - God's Word says: you have enough power

Jesus said, "You shall have power in the coming of the Holy Spirit, and you shall be my witnesses." (Act.s 1: 8)

Many say: I have not enough courage - God's Word says: you can get more

"The congregation prayed for Peter and John. They prayed: And now, Lord, watch their threats, and let your servants speak your word with all boldness.

As you extend your hand to healing and to the signs and wonders of your saint, Jesus serves the name. " (Acts. 4, 29-30)

"Paul and Barnabas preach. They stayed there for a long time, speaking boldly in the Lord, who gave testimony to his word of grace as he showed signs and wonders at their hands.
" (Acts. 14: 3)

"And when Paul laid his hands on them, the Holy Spirit came upon them, and they spoke with tongues and prophetic words.

These men were a total of about twelve.

Paul spoke boldly in the synagogue – boldness brings results

He then entered the synagogue and spoke boldly for three months, holding conversations with them and convincing them of what belongs to the kingdom of God.

But when someone hardened himself and refused to believe, and spoke badly of God's way so the crowd listened to it, he broke with them and separated their disciples, and held daily conversations in the school of Tyrannus.

This lasted for two years, so that all who lived in Asia heard the word of the Lord, both Jews and Greeks.

And extraordinary works of God did by Paul's hands,

So that they even took sweat cloths or aprons that he had worn and carried to the sick, and the diseases departed from them, and the evil spirits brought out of them. " (Acts 19: 6-12)

"The wicked flee without anyone pursuing them, but the righteous are bold, bold as the young lion." (Proverbs 28, 1, King James)

Without boldness no result

Based on these verses and the experiences they hold, we clearly see that "the power of preaching of faith" without boldness is "the power of theology of faith". It will only be a lot of big empty words. The words are not filled with the power until you are bold enough to believe them. That is, act on the words, yes, do the words. You have to put the words into practical exercise in the physical world.

To Africa with faith, power and boldness

This has also been my overall experience from the first time I traveled to Africa as a young man. I had been born again, baptized in the Holy Spirit and baptized in water. This happened within a month in February 1973.

I immediately started praying for the sick, casting out evil spirits also came on the field after only a few months.

The necessity of boldness

I clearly saw what was a necessity along with faith and power. I had to dare to believe the promises of the Word of God, I had to dare to believe that the power I had received in the baptism of the Holy Spirit.

I trusted in God's word, as it said it was. I went on with great boldness.

The results did not wait

I experienced many results when it came to healing and deliverance right from the start as a Christian.

After 2 years as a Christian, I was 22 and ready for my first trip to the Third World. First trip to Kenya in East Africa. From my very first encounter in the Third World, miracles and signs were and under a strong fact. This has been the case in all meetings without exception for over 40 years.

Jesus' victory on Calvary stands firm forever
Every conscious that you have the power, every conscious that you have the faith and use the boldness as strongly as you can. It's just getting started.

God's Word creates two things - signs, wonders and miracles and resistance

"In Jesus Christ our Lord, in whom we have our boldness and access with confidence through faith in Him." (Eph. 3:12)

"Paul said: By my heartfelt longing and my hope that I should not be ashamed of anything, but that Christ, as always, now and now, with all boldness be glorified in my body, whether it be alive, or death." (Phil 1:20)

"And all who will live godly in Christ Jesus shall be persecuted." (2 Tim 3, 12)

Jesus said to the disciples in his farewell speech, "If they have persecuted me, they too shall persecute you." (John. 15:20)

Are you willing to walk with Christ in faith, power and boldness
If you want to do that, your opponents will be there and so will the victories of Christ Jesus.
The victory in Christ Jesus will be there in you.
You have been born into the winning team.

13

Touch the hearts of the world

"And my speech and preaching was not with the persuasive words of wisdom, but with the evidence of Spirit and power,

So that their faith should not be based on the wisdom of men but on the power of God. "
(1 Cor. 2: 4)

It is not enough to talk about the kingdom - we must prove the kingdom
We are the producers of evidence, the royal proclaimers. See yourself in that position.

"Jesus said: But tell me by the Spirit of God that I cast out the evil spirits, then the kingdom of God has come to you." (Matt. 12:28)

122

You are the catalyst and portal
Do you see it, the power of God's kingdom from the spiritual world, to materialize through you, to be brought into the physical world by you? You are the catalyst and portal into the planet earth.

"And in Lystra sat a man who had no power in his feet, when he was disfigured from the womb, and who could never walk.

He heard Paul's speech, which looked sharply at him, and when he saw that he had faith to be healed, he said with a loud voice:

Stand upright on your feet. And he jumped up and walked around.

But when the people saw what Paul had done, they cried with a loud voice in Lyaconic, saying: The gods have become like men, and have come down to us." (Acts. 14: 8-11)

Where you are is the power of the Kingdom of God. You can have the forces of the fourth dimension, the forces of the Spirit of God manifest on earth, which is a planet subject to the 3-dimensional laws. The planet where you live from your senses.

That is what Jesus commanded his disciples to do.

Hear what Jesus says to the disciples.

"And as you depart, preach this message: The kingdom of heaven is at hand.

Heal the sick, raise the dead, clean the lepers, expel evil spirits. For nothing have you received it, for nothing you will give it. " (Matt. 10, 7-8)

The demons are manifesting themselves
Demons always begin to manifest in the meetings I have. They begin to manifest as I stand and talk. Then I get the helpers who help take them out of the crowd and take them behind the platform. There they cast the demons out of them. There are also other ways I do it. The situation is completely different. When I come to the meetings, I always expect the manifestations of the demons and the sick begin to heal.

Let the forces of the fourth dimension be brought to you by the world
You who are born again are the tools. You have the power, use the faith, use it boldly.

"Jesus said, if you abide in my word, then in truth you are my disciples." (John. 8:31)

"Jesus said more to the disciples, He said: I was with you all the days until the end of the world." (Matt. 28:20)

You can do this in Jesus' name if you are willing to become a true disciple of Jesus. One who has Jesus as Lord in his life.
Jesus is with you through the Holy Spirit. You can take territories in the name of Jesus. You can change the circumstances no matter where you are.

See your circumstances as God sees them
Hear what the Bible says:

"In the beginning was the Word and the Word was with God, and the Word was God."
(John. 1, 1)

This is very simple and understandable
To see what God sees is to see what God's Word says.

"But we who, with an unseen face, behold the glory of the Lord as in a mirror, we are all transformed into the same image from glory to glory, as by the Spirit of the Lord." (2 Cor. 3: 18)
It's like looking in the mirror
What a fantastic statement by Paul in his letter to the Corinthians. This simple explanation gives you a revelation of this reality.
As you eagerly study God's written Word and obey God's written Word, you will gradually become more and more like God's Word.
It's like looking in the mirror. You become like what you see - written or what you experience from the fulfillment of the promises of the Word of God, when you step into it in the bold belief that God's power is in you and with you in the name of Jesus.

Let the kingdom power flow from the temple
"Do you not know that your bodies are a temple of the Holy Spirit, dwelling within you, and

which you have from God, and that you do not belong to yourself? (1 Cor 6:19)

"Whoever believes in me as the scripture has said, out of his heart shall flow rivers of kingdom water." (John. 7, 38)

If you do your part, God will fulfill it, it will go completely automatically
You see, it's in you, just go with it. You do not need to pray and pray, you do not need any special assurances from God, nor do you get it. It will just something you possibly imagine you got. You have the written Word of God. If you fulfill your part as a disciple of Jesus Christ, God fulfills His part. When all parts are in the right place, it works.

Give the world what you want its calling

"Jesus said, if you abide in me and my words abide in you, pray for what you want and you will receive it." (John. 15:17)

"But have pleasure in the law of the Lord, and consider his law day and night.

He will be like a tree planted by flowing streams, which will yield its fruit in its time, and if the leaves do not wither, and everything he does, he shall be successful. " (Psalm 1, 2 - 3)

Do you see? If your life is in the right place with the Lord, the power of God will flow through you.

You are God's best - give it to your neighbor - worldwide
"And this gospel of the kingdom shall be preached throughout the whole kingdom to a testimony (martyrdom) for all peoples, and then shall the end come." (Matt. 24:14)

The power of death is broken - Let God's dream of love flow through you into a longing world.

To what kind of people did Jesus give this great command?

"Jesus said, Go out into all the world and preach the gospel to all creation." (Mark. 16, 15)

Read verses 16 to 19 as well. I have them and a little earlier in the book. They contain the tools to accomplish this task of God, which is to all of us without exception.

If we take a look at verse 14, we see what kind of people Jesus gave this command to first. It was Jesus' disciples who had hidden away and were terrified. Satan called into your mind and said: Now they have taken Jesus, now they will take you too. Hear what the verse says:

"But at last he revealed himself to the eleven himself, but they sat down to table, and he punished them for their unbelief and hard hearts, because they had not believed those who had seen him rise." (Mark. 16:14)

Look at the disciples and look at yourself
Do you see the opportunities you have? The disciples were simple people, as we all are. If Jesus could use these, he can and will use you.
Get to the position and you're in the progression.

We are God's tools
Believe that the power of God has been lost in you since you were born again, became a new

creature, and baptized in the Holy Spirit. If this is not true, then God would not have said:

"If you confess with your mouth Jesus as Lord, and believe in your heart that God raised Him from the dead, then you will be saved."
(Rom. 10: 9)

Zoe

The word saved is called in English saved. In Norwegian, this means saved. From Greek to Norwegian it means "saved to spirit, soul, and body. This is the reality of your new life in Christ.

God has made everything possible in your life, so that you are able to do what He asks you to do, only you are in position with your life, you decide for yourself.

God would never ask you to do something you were unable to do.

"He has done everything in his day though, also eternity (the world, the cosmos) he has put their heart into, but so that man cannot fully understand the work God has done, from beginning to end." (Ecclesiastes 3, 11)

"By grace, you are saved, by faith, and it is not of yourselves, it is a gift of God." (Eph. 2: 8)

You see, the possibilities for doing the impossible are in you.
It means from God that God is ready if you are ready.
The world is waiting for you, the world is waiting for God's powerful men, people who bring the Kingdom with you, you can be one of them.

Go and touch the heart of the world
People will love you, the precious people for whom Jesus gave His life. God is still God, so go touch the hearts of the world.

1 4

You are God's voice to the world

"And the Lord shall guide you at all times and saturate you amid in the wilderness; and your bones shall he strengthen; (Jes. 58:11)

"Jesus said: Whoever believes in me as the scripture has said, out of his life shall flow streams of living water.

This He said of the Spirit that they should receive who believed in Him, for the Spirit had not yet come, because Jesus was not yet glorified." (John 7, 38-39)

God wants His Spirit materialized today, through you. You are God's voice to the world today
The Atonement is complete, the victory is passed on to you. Christ wants you to be part of the completion of His command with the power of

the Holy Spirit and the use of the tools He has given you for the task in His name, in Jesus name. This is well explained in Mark 16, 15-19.

You are God's messenger, where you are, Christ is in you and through you
"How beautiful on the mountains are its feet that come with glad tidings, who preach peace, who carry good news, who preach salvation."
(Jes. 52: 7)

What a privilege. Imagine being a messenger with life. The life of Christ pulsating over your lips to a dying world. Where you come, eternal life comes through you through the Holy Spirit in the wonderful name of Jesus.

To the extent that his divine nature is in you, you will be his mouth
"Since his divine power has given us everything that serves life and godliness, through the knowledge of him who called us by his own glory and power.

And thereby have given us the greatest and most precious promises, that by them ye may be partakers of the Divine nature… "(2 Peter 1, 3 - 4)

God's eternal nature in you, is called "eternal life"

"Jesus said: The devil comes only to steal, murder, and destroy, but I have come for them to have life and to have abundance." (John. 10:10)

This life is God, God creates opportunities, which God manifested through the creation and has given to us.
The miracle-working power is given to us in Jesus name.

"By faith we understand that the world is made by the word of God, so that what is seen was not made manifest." (Heb. 11, 3)

Reflect on what is given to you in Christ.

The creative opportunity as seen in creation is now available to us, following the written word of God. This is available to the new creature.

The Gentile nations do not have it

They exist on planet earth with no hope beyond
their limited existence.

"Remember that you were pagans as before ...

That at that time you stood outside Christ ... ...
alien to the covenant with its promises, without
hope and without God in the world; "
(Eph. 2, 11-12)

Let your voice help people

You are God's voice to the world. The world dies
if we don't give it life. You are God's miracle
man. You can give the world the miracle it
needs. It is in your spirit; you can let it flow out
of your mouth.
Let your voice help people.

It works - the hope of the Gentiles is in you

You don't stand up to people with something you
"hope" works. You are God's voice, God's life to
the world and you know it.

"But now in Christ Jesus, ye that are far off are
come nigh unto the blood of Jesus Christ."

(Eph. 2: 13)

"For God so loved the world that he gave his only begotten Son, that whosoever believeth in him should not perish, but have everlasting life." (John 3:16)
"Jesus says, that whoever believes in Jesus will have eternal life.

God did not send His Son into the world to judge the world, but for the world to be saved, through Him.

Whoever believes in him will not be judged;
" (John. 3, 15,17,18)

God's life is in you and you know it
You give life to the Gentiles, you give it the eternal reality of hope. You give recognition victory. (Ecclesiastes 3, 11)

 They come close to Christ because of His eternally victorious holy blood. The victory that he won at Calvary cross over all the empire of Satan once and for all eternity, (John. 19, 28 - 34)

Listen to this verse, it's up to you
"And they triumphed over him, Satan, and the
demons, by the blood of the Lamb, of Jesus, and
the words which he testified (martyrdom); and
they had not loved their lives, even to death.
" (Rev. 12, 11)

**You see - because of Jesus you have the life of
God in you**

As Jesus said, you can say: I am from God.

"But when John in prison heard of the works of
Christ, he sent with his disciples, saying unto Jesus,

Are you the one to come, or should we wait for
another?

And Jesus answering said unto them, Go, tell
John what ye hear and see:

The blind see and the lame walk, the lepers are
cleansed and the deaf hear and the dead rise, and
the gospel is preached to the poor;"
(Matt. 11, 2 - 5)

As one sent from God, these signs will follow you
And as you depart, preach this message: The kingdoms of heaven have come nigh!

Heal the sick, raise the dead, for nothing you have received, for nothing shall you give it.
" (Matt 10, 1 and 7 -8)

"Jesus said to the Jews who had come to believe in him: If you abide in my word, then you are truly my disciples" (John 8:31).

If the Bible is the governing word in our lives, then we are Jesus' disciples, then we are sent by God. The victory Jesus won is then given to us in His name for the exercise of us.

"Jesus came forward and said, 'All power has been given to me in heaven and on earth;

Therefore go out and make all peoples my disciples " (matt. 28, 18 - 19)

Do you see what you have and who you are in Christ?

You can say: I am a conqueror in Christ

Isn't it wonderful, when only our spiritual eyes are opened to these realities and lead to our natural understanding? An understanding in our human mind, in the three-dimensional physical world.

Hear God's Word and Do It.

"You are of God my children, and you have overcome them, for he who is in you is greater than he who is in the world." (1 John. 4, 4)

The scriptures say further
"For all that is born of God overcomes the world, and this is the victory that overcometh the world, our faith." (1 John. 5, 4)

You were born to win

The secret to "living life" and "being in the word of God" is that you can stand up for the world we live in, as a winner, you can stand as "Gods overcomes son" "Although I am never that human, I still do not fight with human weapons

Over wapons

For our weapons of war are not carnal, sensuous,
but in the power of God they are powerful
enough to bring down all the fortifications of the
enemy,

I can knock down every fortification of thought
buildings (knowledge of senses) and any height
that rises against the knowledge of God (knowledge of revelation) and capture every thought
(sense of knowledge) under obedience to Christ"
(2 Cor. 10, 3-5).
which is then again against God's written word.

This surprises many, they have not seen it, they
have not read it, they have not understood it,
what they have in Christ.
But we have that now.

"The word is near to you, in your mouth and in
your heart (spirit), that is the word of faith, that
which we preach." (Rom. 10: 8)

"By the way - be strong in the Lord and in the
power of His might!

Put on the full armor of God so that you can stand against the devil's cunning attack;

For we are not fighting against flesh and blood, but against powers, against authorities, against the rulers of the darkness of this world, against the evil armies in high places, that is in the spiritual world, Cosmos.

I write more details about this in some of my other books, one of them are In the spirit.

Therefore, put on the full armor of God so that you can resist the evil day and stand after overcoming everything.

Then stand girded about their loins with truth, and clothed with the armor of righteousness,

And bound on their feet with the skill of battle that the gospel of peace provides,

And grasp, besides all this shield of faith, by which you shall be able to extinguish all the fiery arrows of evil,

And take the helmet of salvation and the sword
of the Spirit, which is the word of God,

As you pray in the Spirit at all times with all
prayer and invocation and are vigilant therein
with all endurance and prayer for all the saints,

And also for me, that I must give words when I
open my mouth, that I may boldly proclaim the
secret of the gospel, "(Eph. 6: 10-19).

"And they, the Trinity, the Word) have triumphed
over him, Satan, by the blood of the Lamb and
the words they witnessed (martyr)."
(Rev. 12, 11)

"He, Jesus, disarmed the powers and the authorities and openly displayed them, showing them,
as the Lord of victory over them, Satan and the
demons, on the cross." (Col. 2, 15)

"Therefore, saith the LORD of hosts: Behold, I
will make my words in your mouth a fire."
(Jer. 5, 14)

"But he (the word) who can do more than anything, far beyond what we ask or understand, according to the power that becomes in us"
(Eph. 3:20).

"And behold, I am with you all days until the
end of the world." (Matt. 28:20)

15

"Miracle faith" requires action

Believe the word, act on the word, that's what we have to do, then the Lord will automatically act through you and me. It is the very simple principles of faith that must be done, the results are not you or I responsible for, it is the Lord's responsibility. When you understand the Lord's promises, you dare and believe it. You go past the dare and say I think so. We all have a way to go here, just get started, all things have a start.

Mountain base
"Therefore, whoever hears these my words and does (believe) after them, he becomes like a wise man who builds his house on the mountains.

And the rains fell and the flood came, and the wind blew and struck this house, but it did not fall, because it was founded on mountains.
" (Matt 7, 24-25)

He who hears must become a doer, one who believes what he reads and says.

Sand base

"And whoever hears my words and does not obey them, becomes like a foolish man who builds his house on sand;

And the rains fell, and the flood came, and the wind blew and struck this house, and it fell, and its fall was great! " (Matt. 7, 26 - 27)

True, it was he who only trusted what the senses told. Here there was no faith in the word of the Lord. He did not act on what he heard, and the fall was great. There is always a choice and the choice is yours. It goes to fall or victory.

"But be the doer of the word, and not the hearer of the word only, in that you deceive yourself.

For if one is the hearer of the word and not the doer of it, he is like unto a man that looketh on his natural countenance in a mirror;

The doer and proclaimer of the word

Anyone who believes that knowledge of the senses is what brings victory will fail. It is the doers of the Word, those who believe the Word, those who practice the Word, who live the promises of the Word. Those who walk their lives in it are the ones who build the truths of the word as bearers for their lives, that is, they will honor God.

Producers of Evidence

This is evidence of the producers of Jesus' resurrection from the dead. It is these who prove that Christ Jesus is the very Son of God.

These are the ones standing on the barricades in front of the Gentiles with the gospel of peace to health, salvation, and deliverance. The truths of the gospel must slowly but surely be built into you with the faith of revelation knowledge. Little by little, the spiritual proclaimer of faith emerges.

Spiritual or carnal

The spiritual senses are sharp and respond spiritually with God's written words as a guide in one and all. Here it responds faster than it does through sense knowledge, this act with divine power and insight. This has become natural to you. You have got an automatically respond to the spiritual realities through the word. Here it moves spiritually and with carnality subject, whereas sense knowledge only responds to the carnal.

We are not in the prison of sense knowledge
The one who limits throughout life to what the natural senses show us. We are in the freedom of revelation knowledge. We have the knowledge of the senses like everyone else, but we have another unlimited sense. We have the spiritual sense of God Jehovah. We have God's spiritual senses of God, which are boundless. We go all over the cosmos. The Word, the Spirit, and the faith are our guides to eternal life, the nature of God.

Sense knowledge limit – Revelation knowledge, Gods spirit release eteral eternity.

Sense knowledge
imits your area to what you are able to record with your senses geographically

Revelation knowledge

Is boundless, it covers what God covers. The cosmos and beyond into eternity, it is the geographical area of the Holy Spirit.

One can deceive oneself

You know the Bible's words, you know Greek and Hebrew. You can know the Bible's historical facts. Everything will be of no use to you unless the Word of the Bible lives in you and you practice it, yes believe it.

Live in victory anyway

When God's Word has become as much a part of your personality as your circumstances are, you are approaching where God wants you to be. Now you need to train yourself to respond to the life of God through the word in you, just as you have always reacted to signals through your natural senses.

A disciple of Jesus

Living in victory will always lead to conflicts It is to learn, to be a disciple of Jesus. Even if the circumstances around you are against you, you live in victory. Because you have trained your spiritual senses to become stronger than your physical senses. This means that you react to the circumstances automatically, with what God's Word says about any situation / event. The Word of God in you today always becomes what has the last word and is the victorious, not what your physical senses tell you. This is to live in victory. Living in victory will always bring conflicts to the field.

We live in a spiritual war
We live in a spiritual war, so whoever lives in victory will always have opposition from the world of sensory knowledge. I have worked as a nurse in between all my service to the Lord for all years. In the workplaces at different hospitals, I have always had reactions to who I am, without saying a single word. What you are and what you have cannot be hidden. There will be reactions that in some cases will create conflicts.

It will always be this way when your life is established in victory. It is a knowledge that is important to bring in this context.

"Don't go in disbelief"

I will include some verses for you in this context
"Do not go in a foreign yoke with disbelief! For what harm do justice have, or what society has light with darkness?

And what harmony is there between Christ and Belial, or what fate and part does a believer have with an infidel?
And what is the consensus between God's temple and idols? After all, we are the temple of the living God, as God has said: I will dwell among them and travel among them, and I will be their God, and they shall be my people. "
(2 Cor. 6: 14-16)

Protect Your Vulnerability

We see Paul exhorting the Corinthians to separate from paganism. We must be aware that we are natural people, we are very vulnerable. Precisely for that reason, it is of the utmost importance that we do as Paul exhorts, to separate ourselves from paganism.

What you paid a high price for with your own life - don't let anyone take it from you

What you have paid a high price for with life, do not let anyone take it from you. Protect it with your life. The closer you get to fellowship with God, the more you will feel the importance of having contact with Him and less contact with what sense of knowledge has to present to you.

The treasure we have is in camps
"For God, who commanded that light shine forth out of darkness, he is the one who also made it shine in our hearts, that the knowledge of the glory of God in the sight of Jesus Christ might shine forth from us.
But we have this treasure in camps, that the mighty power may be of God and not of us"
(2 Cor. 4, 6 - 7)
The strength we have in Christ must be carefully protected so that it is not harmed. We have the treasure in our fragile earthenware, which is our personality and body, which are so easily influenced. Remember that you are a tool in God's hand, take good care of it, and be careful with the tool, so it may be in God's honor what it is meant to be.
"No weapon forged against you shall prosper, and every tongue that goeth against you shall be

condemned; this is the heritage of the servants of the Lord, and the right which they shall receive of me," saith the Lord. (Isa. 54:17)

You can trust the Lord

We do not beg in the world of sensory knowledge, we do not depend on the world of sensory knowledge. We believe the word, we do the word in practice. We live the word; we trust the word. Listen to what the following verse says.

God is love

"Jesus said: Just as the Father has loved me, so have I loved you, so be in my love."
(John. 15: 9)

" God is love." (John. 4: 8)

"Have given us the greatest and most precious promises, that by them ye may be partakers of Divine nature." (2 Peter 1, 4)

Work your spiritual life forward

The Divine nature, the nature of love, it is yours in Christ Jesus. In a quiet trust in God, you live out this love, you practice it. You don't just talk about it. T.L.Osborn said it so wonderfully. He said: play the love of it wins your whole personality. This is true of all spiritual parts in us, practice them. Work on them again and again, until they sit, until they become part of you, until they become you, until you become what God wants you to be for Him. Let nothing outside you interfere with your spiritual development. " Do not go in unbelief."

"A new commandment I give unto you, that ye love one another, as I have loved you, ye also love one another." (John. 13, 34)

The word "Like" in this Bible verse is meant to be"practiced".

Often misunderstood

Walking in God's love is an often-misunderstood statement. It is often handled in a very invisible way. Eros is the physical pursuit, Agape is the divine pursuit of what we have the word love for. When you live the love life, it is Jesus who has gained a place in your life. It is because of Him in you, that you have that love in you. Then you will begin to act and love as Jesus did.

"Jesus said, I am the light of the world; he that follow me shall not walk in darkness but have the light of life." (John. 8:12)

You have to prove to the world that you have the light

He who walks in human reason walks in the dark. They don't know where they are going. They have deceived themselves. Healthy teachings are just teachings to them. For them, it is only creed of empty theological words. They agree that the Bible is true, but they do not agree if you ask them to live it practically.
Those who love Jesus and have His love in them will not deceive anyone. Those who are the hearers of the word, but not the doers of the word, are good talkers, yes speakers. They are not the doers of the word and can, therefore, deceive many.

"Jesus said: I am the vine, you are the branches, he who abides in me and I in him, he bears much fruit, for without me you can do nothing.

154

If anyone does not stay in me, he is thrown out like a branch that withers, and they are sunk together and thrown into the fire, and they burn.

"If you stay in me and my words stay in you, ask for what you want and you will get it."
(John 15: 5-7)

I am the light of the world; he that follow me shall not walk in darkness but have the light of life." (John. 8:12)

What kind of fruit is this?
Here it is talking about the fruit of love, the fruit is believed, the bean fruit. This is the same kind of fruit that Jesus had. Now, this same fruit of love works through Christ in you, as it did through Christ as he physically walked here on planet earth.

Listen to this verse, "By this, my Father is glorified, that ye bear much fruit". (John 15: 8)

Those who only hear can quote many correct promises but do not have life in the world, in the promises. Only those who believe, who "do" the word, release a ripe fruit.

I'll take another verse again. " If you stay in me and my words stay in you, pray for what you want and you will get it. " (John 15: 5-7)

Jesus Christ your absolutely Lord

Christ is the Word. If we let the Word become Lord in our lives, that is, we stay in Him, and His Word remains in us, and we allow the Word to do its work with our lives, then we can ask what we want and we will get it.
Then it is no longer a doctrine, but God speaks and lives in His word in us and through us, to the world around us. This only start when Jesus has really become the Jesus has become Lord in your life.

"And will you know that you poor man, that faith without works (actions) is useless." (James 2:20)

If you do not act on the word, you are no believer in it either. Then you are only a human being with a Bible. You evaluate the Bible's words based on human reason without action. Then it's just empty words and religion.

Jesus called it "building houses on sand."
(John. 7:26)

"But he that hath the goods of the world, and seeth his brother, is crushed, and shut his heart unto him, how can the love of God abide in him?

My children, let us not love with words or with tongues, but with deeds (actions) and truth. "
(1 John. 3, 17-18)

How does God's love work?
Does it work because of studies in the word? Does it work because of all our knowledge of it in the word? Does it work without us living the word? No it doesn't. Let's do, believe, act on love, assuming we have become love. We have become products of love in Christ. Release the love of Christ in you.

Love carries the light, you are guided by love

"And this is the message that we have heard
from him and preach to you, that God is light,
and there is no darkness in him.

If we say we have fellowship with Him and walk
in the market, then we are lying and not doing
the truth. " (1 John. 1, 5 - 6)"
Then it is no longer a doctrine, but God speaks
and lives in His word in us and through us, to the
world around us.

"And will you know that your poor man, that
faith without works (actions) is useless."
(James 2:20)

If you do not act on the word, you are no believer in it either. Then you are only a human being
with a Bible. You evaluate the Bible's words
based on human reason without action. Then it's
just empty words and religion.

Jesus called it "building houses on sand."
(John. 7:26)

"But he that hath the goods of the world, and seeth his brother, is crushed, and shut his heart unto him, how can the love of God abide in him?

My children, let us not love with words or with tongues, but with deeds (actions) and truth. "
(1 John. 3, 17-18)

And upon this we shall know that we are of the truth, and then we shall satisfy our hearts before him;

For if our heart condemns us, God is greater than our heart and knows all things.

You beloved! If our heart does not condemn us, then we have boldness for God,

And what we ask for, we get from him; because we keep his commandments and do what pleases him. " (1 John 3, 19-23)

We must always search our hearts and be honest with God. Tell him you are walking the path of love. He knows if you do, but say it anyway. He wants to hear the consciousness from your mouth. Make the Word of God alive over your lips. Let God use your lips. Let's be "God pleasers," Jesus it was.

"But the Comforter of the Holy Ghost, whom the Father shall send in my name, he shall teach you all things, and remind you of all things which I have told you." (Jn 14:26)

"We are God's people." (1 Cor. 3: 9)

"If God is for us, then who is against us." (Rom. 8: 1)

You work and do not act on the word alone; we cooperate with God all the way. He will follow you up every step you take.

Love gives us eternal strength and victory
"That he, God, according to the riches of his glory, may give you to be strengthened with power by his Spirit in the inward man,

That Christ must live by faith in their hearts,

So that you rooted and rooted in love, must be able to grasp with all the saints what breadth and length and depth and height there are,

And know the love of Christ, which surpasses all knowledge, that you may be filled to the fullness of God. " (Eph. 3: 16-19)

You see eternity's eternity full of all God has for you through love.
God does nothing for you, but He does it through you to the world around you.

1 6

Give life and speech revelation

"Jesus said, I am the way of truth and life."
(Jn 14, 6)

Jesus Christ holds all the possibilities of revelation to you, Jesus is the perfect will of God.

"Jesus said: The devil comes only to steal, murder, and destroy; hunters have come to give you life and life in abundance." (John. 10:10)

"We know that we have passed from death to life, because we love the brothers, the one who does not love, remains in death.

In this we know the love that he set his life for us, also we are guilty of putting life to the brothers. " (1 John. 3, 14-16)

We must become Jesus people, people who give life to people.
People who speak and proclaim revelation of God's perfect will.
The moment you speak revelation, people will accept and believe what you say.

"But Peter said, I have no silver and gold, but what I have I give you, in the name of Jesus Christ, get up and walk." (Acts 3: 6)

Peter said: what I have, what he was conscious he had received from Christ. He had no New Testament, but he was a demonstration of it, as you should be.

"Jesus said: You shall have power in the coming of the Holy Spirit, and you shall be my witnesses (martyrs, proof-makers) throughout Judea and Samaria, and even to the outermost and most distant places, the ends of the earth." (Acts 1: 8)

Let "life" live in you
Peter let Jesus' "life" reign in him, Peter then became the revelation of Christ and God's will to

his world. He was a Jesus person, a witness a martyr (proof producer) that you too can be.

You are first and foremost a witness

"Therefore, one of the men who walked with us all the time the Lord Jesus went in and out of us, Right from his baptism at John until the day he was admitted from us - one of these should witness with us his resurrection. " (Acts. 1, 21-22)

Certain qualifications a witness had to have

Here the disciples chose one who had walked with them during Jesus' time on earth. They chose one who had seen the gospel in flesh and blood in its entirety on earth. We do not have the gospel in flesh and blood, but we do have the written gospel, the Bible Word of God. If we live according to it, then we are a witness. Jesus was their New Testament, we have the written New Testament. We have not walked with Jesus physically, but we have His will and descriptions of His life. But today, as they then, the gospel is passed on as a "witness."

His will

"Jesus said, For I have come down from heaven, not to do my will, but to do his will which sent me." (John. 6, 38)

His life

"For the Word of God is alive and powerful and sharper than any twisted sword and penetrates, until it closes the soul and spirit, the guts and the margins, and judges the thoughts and counsel of the heart." (Heb 4, 12)

"In the beginning was the Word, and the Word was with God, and the Word was God."
(John. 1, 1)

"The Word became flesh and dwelt among us, and we saw His glory - a glory which the only begotten Son hath of his Father - full of grace and truth." (John. 1:14)

For they are the life of everyone that find them, and the cure of the whole body of men

Keep your heart (spirit) above all that is preserved, for life is based on it. "

(Proverbs 4, 20 - 23)

"And they, you and me, triumphed over him, the devil, by virtue of the blood of the Lamb, Jesus, and the words it testified (Martyrdom, proof-makers, revealed God's will, from Greek)" (Revelation 12:11).

"But at last he revealed himself to the eleven as they sat at the table, and he punished them for their unbelief and hard hearts because they had not believed those who had seen him rise.

And he said to them: Go out into all the world (Cosmos Greek / Hebrew) and preach the gospel to all creation!

He who believes and is baptized shall be saved, but he that believeth not shall be damned.

And these signs shall follow them that believe: In my name shall they cast out devils, they shall speak with tongues;

They will take snakes at the ends, and if they drink something poisonous, it will not harm them; they shall lay their hands upon the sick, and they shall be healed. Then, after he had spoken to them, a Lord Jesus was taken to heaven and sat down at the right hand of God.

But they went out and preached the word everywhere, and the Lord acted and confirmed the word by the signs that came. " (Mark. 16, 14-20)

"If you abide in my word, then you are truly my disciples," (John. 8:31).

Jesus is never more Lord in our lives than the written Word of God is Lord in our lives. Jesus is the Word (John 1: 1)

"If you stay in me and my words stay in you, ask for what you want and you will get it." (John. 15: 7)

"And behold I am with you all the days, until the end of the age." (Matt. 28:20)

Everything has been arranged for you.

1 7

Break loose - The Lord is watching you

"And these signs shall follow him that believeth, In my name shall they cast out devils, they shall speak with tongues;

They will take snakes in their hands, and if they drink something poisonous, it will not harm them;

In sick they shall lay their hands, and they shall be healed. " (Mark. 16, 17-18)

There are certain criteria that must be in place in a person's life before "before these signs shall follow whoever believes" may come into operation. Let's take a look at who the believers are.

Who are the believers?

"All that is born of God overcomes the world, and this is the victory that overcomes the world, our faith." (1 John. 5, 4)

Here we quickly see that there is talk of a "new birth" to get this kind of "faith" which is called "our faith". Then the question becomes, who is born of God?

Who is born of God?

"All who received him, Jesus, gave him the right to become children of God, those who believe in his name.

And they are born, not of blood, nor of the will of the flesh, nor of the will of man, but of God. " (John. 1: 12-13)

According to what you are now reading, all those who received Jesus are born again. I have a question here. In what way should we receive Jesus? This is what the Bible has a clear statement about, we take it.

In what way should we receive Jesus?

There is a Bible site that explains this easily.
This is the letter of Romans we read from there.

"If you confess with your mouth Jesus as Lord,
and believe in your heart that God raised him
from the dead, then you will be saved."
(Rom. 10: 9)

No. 1 is that you let Jesus become Lord in your
life. Jesus never becomes Lord in your life, more
than the written Word of God becomes Lord in
your life. If you are willing to let the written
Word of God be Lord in your life and rule your
entire life, then you have met the first criterion.

No. 2 You must believe that God raised Christ
from the dead. The belief in this is embedded in
your soul from creation so that you can just
make the choice you are facing right now. Do
you spend your life willingly and say and believe with all your heart that you believe God
raised Christ from the dead. Then you do it.

Now you have met both of the criteria to be
saved, which means being saved from the sin of

inheritance by being born again. You are born again in your inner man, in your spirit. Hear what the Bible says so wonderfully.

"Therefore, if anyone in Christ has been saved, then he is a new creature. The old is gone, see everything has become new. " (2 Cor. 5: 17)

Now you have that belief in your mind, in your spirit, that can produce the characters that I mentioned in the beginning of the chapter.

 "Without anyone being born again, he cannot see the Kingdom of God." (John. 3, 3)

"What is born of the Spirit is spirit." (John. 3: 6)

"God is spirit." (John. 4, 24)

You have become a citizen of heaven, like the new creature you have become. Fantastic, you've been born again.

What are you? Who are born of God?

"You have been justified in the name of the Lord Jesus and in the Spirit of our God." (1 Cor. 6:11)

"The righteous are as bold as the young lion." (Proverbs 28, 1)

You as the born-again are the bold one, it is in you. Dare to stand up believing you are and live it. You don't see it, you don't feel it, but the boldness is there in your spirit - release it in the name of Jesus.

"Paul also said, Pray also for me, that I must speak when I open my mouth, that I may boldly proclaim the secret of the gospel." (Eph. 6:19)

It is amazing to stand in front of people with the gospel. Stand there and know with certainty that the Lord is opening the secret of the gospel to those who hear. It is powerful. Paul had this boldness and we have it. Release it in you. Listen to this.

Peter and John were imprisoned and placed before the councilors. They could not but tell the truths about their experiences with the risen Christ Jesus.

"Then it shall be evident unto you all, and to all the people of Israel, that by the name of Jesus Christ, the Nazarene, whom ye crucified, whom God raised from the dead, by him is this healing before your eyes.

He is the stone that was rejected by you, you builders, but which has become the cornerstone.

And there is no salvation in anyone else; for there is no other name under heaven given among men by which we shall be saved.

But when they saw the boldness of Peter and John, and learned that they were unlearned and healing men, they marveled, and they recognized them, that they had been with Jesus; And when they saw the man standing by their side, the one who had been healed, they could not resist.
" (Acts. 4: 10-14)

"When they were now released, they came to their own and told them all the high priests and the elders had told them.

When they heard this, they unanimously lifted their voice to God and said, Lord! You who made heaven and earth and the sea and all that is in it, " (Acts. 4: 23-24)

Religious people do not like boldness, they are terrified of it, it challenges you. It wants you to do what you say you are. If we live surrendered to Christ, wisdom, and love will grow and be dominant in our lives.

"The church which is the body of Christ is filled with him who fills everything in everyone."
(Eph. 1: 23)

That's what we're part of.

"I can do everything in him that makes me strong." (Philip. 4, 13)

Do you see who you are in Christ? Don't be scared, it's you in Him. Dare to be who you are in Him.

Boldness primarily produces three things - Signs, Wonders and Miracles Here, what happened when Paul boldly proclaimed.

"He then entered the synagogue and spoke boldly for three months, holding conversations with them and convincing them of what belongs to the kingdom of God.

And extraordinary works of God did by Paul's hands,

So that they even took sweat cloths or aprons that he had worn and carried to the sick, and the diseases departed from them, and the evil spirits brought out of them. " (Acts. 19, 8 and 11-12)

The word boldness - boldness was used over and over again. They used
"The boldness of a young lion" (Proverbs 28, 1)

Listen "For my deep desire and hope that I should not be ashamed of anything, but that Christ, as always, now and now, with all boldness, be glorified in my body, whether by life or death." (Philip. 1:20)

"Christ Jesus our Lord, in whom we have our boldness and access with confidence through faith in Him." (Eph. 3:12)

Not only did we receive God's faith in the new birth (1 John. 5, 4), we also received God's boldness. We just have to use it, use it in accordance with God's Word, the Bible. Then you will experience real joy and victory in life.

"He, Jesus, who knew not of sin, hath made us sin for us, that we in him might be justified before God." (2 Cor. 5: 21)

Listen to this verse as well.

"Christ Jesus our Lord, in whom we have our boldness and access with confidence through faith in Him." (Eph. 3:12)

We have "boldness" - because we are "justified" God hears us as quickly as he hears Christ.

Christ justified, you, he took away your sin, he cleansed you from the sin of inheritance and gave you a whole new life. You have come to the position where Satan and the demons are subject to you. You have been given authority over him in Christ Jesus. Criticism and persecution will follow you - But signs, wonders and miracles, God in honor and us for good, will also follow you.

You do not ask for justification - you are justified in Christ. You do not ask for faith - You have faith in Christ. You don't ask for boldness and boldness - You have it in Christ

But we can ask for more boldness, courage

"And now the Lord watch their threats, and command your servants to speak your word with all boldness, boldness." (Acts. 4, 29)
"Paul said, but even before we had suffered and had been abused in Philippi, as you know, we nevertheless had the courage, the boldness of our God to speak the gospel of God to you in great strife." (1 Thess. 2,2)

Do not walk on what you see - but on what God's Word says (Heb. 11, 1)

Say it in the dark - victory - You come out into the light Say it in the light - victory - You remain in the light.

"Therefore, do not waste your boldness, boldness having great pay." (Heb. 10, 35)

You can do what you have faith in, what you have the courage and the courage to do. Choose to Break Out - The Lord God Jehovah and his son Jesus Christ through the Holy Spirit are following you.

1 8

Ready to take the world

"You shall know the truth, and the truth shall set you free." (John 8, 32)

"To freedom, Christ has set us free, so stand firm, do not put yourself under the yoke of bondage again." (Gal. 5, 1)

Walk in the freedom you have received in Christ and go for more. Walk in the revelation you have received and go for more.

If only we could see the full depth
"He disarmed the powers and authorities and openly questioned them, appearing as victorious over them (Satan and the demons) on the cross." (Col. 2:15)

179

"And Jesus came and spake unto them, saying,
All power is given unto me in heaven and on
earth;

Therefore, go forth and make all nations a disciple, baptizing them in the name of the Father, the
Son, and of the Holy Ghost;

And teach them to keep everything I've commanded you. And behold, I am with you all days
until the end of the world. " (Matt. 28, 18 - 19)

Everything is subject to us in Jesus Christ.

"But when Jesus entered into Capernaum, a
prince came unto him, saying,

Master! My boy is lying at home and is in pain.

Jesus said to him, I will come and heal him.

But the centurion answered and said, Lord! I'm
too small for you to go under my roof, but just
say a word and my boy will be healed! "
(Matt. 8, 5-10)

The centurion saw more than most Christians today

He understood that what Jesus had - could Jesus give - What Jesus could give would have the captain.

What you see - you have
What you have - you are free in it
What you are free of - you can give
What you can give - can be received by anyone who wants it

Your freedom takes the world

What you see - you have

"You are of God my children, and you have overcome them, for he who is in you is greater than he who is in the world." (John. 4: 4)

Free to set humanity free - Free to give them the life of Jesus Christ

Your thoughts and your words have the power to transform the situations around you. It is the seeds of God that you sow and they bear fruit, according to their kind. Be aware of how much it has cost Christ to make this available to you. Respond with true empathy and yes, to every truth of God's promises as you understand them.

More you understand – more you have got revealed

The more you understand, the more you have been revealed by the Word of God, the more prison walls will fall in your mind and the fullness of Christ in your life will be revealed to the people around you. We must renew our thoughts and break the links that theology has created. We can move forward in the new miracle energy flowing within us as we learn more about God's will for us.

1 9

Free - to set the world free

The full solution for all of us to stand in a service that works is to be totally free. Listen:

"For freedom, Christ has set us free, so stand firm in your freedom, and do not let yourself be left under the yoke of bondage." (Gal. 5: 1)

You are the one with the choice, you will be left at liberty with the opportunity to pass it on.

We read further "If the Son, Jesus Christ, sets you free, then you will be truly free."
(John. 8, 38)

Be willing
Be willing to give your all to Christ Jesus, repent of everything negative in your life. Use your will, to make a true conversion. Let Christ Jesus be your Lord fully. Let the Bible alone be your

Lord, your guide, your instructor. Christ has won the victory for you, the Holy Spirit will guide you in the service of your life to the Lord Jesus Christ.

"Jesus said: but the Comforter, the Holy Ghost, whom the Father shall send in my name, he shall teach you all things, and remind you of all things which I have spoken unto you." (John. 14:26)

Adam and Eve were created in freedom to live in God's dream of freedom They lived the dream in practice until the tragedy happened. They disobeyed God. God's dream of more than enough of everything became a nightmare of lack of all that is good. (Gen. 3: 6). Obedience to God brought in the blessings, but disobedience to God brought in the curses.

The revolution of the victorious world was a fact
"Christ redeemed us from the curse of the law, becoming a curse for us - for it is written, Cursed is every one that hang on a tree." (Gal. 3:13)

Christ won the victory over Satan and the demons. The power of the curse was broken, the blessing and freedom returned.

"Where the Spirit of the Lord is - there is freedom." (2 Cor. 3: 13)

Then walk in the spirit of freedom - How?

We do this by submitting to the written Word of God, which is the same as having Jesus as Lord. Hear.

"In the beginning was the Word, the Word was with God, the Word was God." (John. 1, 1)

We read further, "But he who looks into the perfect law of liberty." (James 1:25)

What is it?
Listen, "But we, as with an unseen face, behold the glory of the Lord as in a mirror; we are all transformed into the same image, from glory to glory, as by the Spirit of the Lord." (2 Cor. 3: 18)

You see, the change begins when the Word becomes your full confidence in your life. You see this is not a difficult composition, but you have to do your part for it to work. It means that Christ will have the opportunity to grow in your life through the living doing of the written Word of God in you.

Get this with you
"He, Jesus must increase in me, I must decrease, of the carnal, the flesh." (John 3:30)

This is a whole process of repentance and a further process of being clothed in the fruits of the Spirit.
Take and read this in Paul's letter to Gal. 5, 15 - 22. I include verse 16

For you. "Paul said, But I say unto you, walk in the Spirit, and ye shall not fulfill the lusts of the flesh (it is that which controls you through your senses)." (Gal. 5, 16)

This is a must-do. If not, the Holy Spirit in our spirit will not have the opportunity to become what it plans to be fully in you, namely Jesus

Christ through you. Through you to the world around you.

Christ wants you free - to set your world free. I'll bring some more Bible verses to you. Imagine the disciples, they received two testimonies of Jesus' resurrection, but they did not believe it, yet ...
He revealed himself to them.

The disciples went from fear to faith
"But at last he revealed himself to the eleven themselves as they sat at table, and he punished them for their unbelief and heart, because they had not believed those who had seen him rise." (Mark. 16:14)

They had been told by two paragraphs already that he was the resurrection, but they did not believe them. So finally, Jesus came in where they were - the resurrection from the dead.

"And Jesus came and spoke unto them, saying, all power is given unto me in heaven and on earth." (Matt. 28:18)

"And Jesus said unto them, go into all the world (cosmos) and preach the gospel to all creation!

And these signs shall follow him that believeth: In my name, in the name of Jesus, they shall cast out demons, they shall speak with tongues; they will take snakes in their hands, and if they drink something poisonous, it will not harm them; on the sick, they will lay their hands and they will be healed. " (Mark. 16, 15-17) "Therefore go out and make all nations a disciple, baptizing them in the name of the Father, and of the Son, and of the Holy Ghost." (Matt. 28:19)

This is the size of your freedom
"You shall know the truth, and the truth shall set you free." (John. 8:32)

Here it was not the knowledge that was the most important, but the knowledge. It was the personal relationship with the Word which is God, who is Christ, who is the Holy Spirit. When the knowledge and experiences become personal in real lifetime after time, a solid close relationship is built with the deity, which in turn gives you a solid freedom of strength you can pass on. What you know and have - you can pass on.

Stephen

Look up your Bible and read Acts 6, 1 and 15, 1, read all the verses, I'll just include two of them here.

v 10) "They were not able to resist the wisdom spoken by Spirit of Stephen.

V 15) "And when all those sitting in the council stared at his face, they saw his face like an angel's face."

Only a strong faith in the new life set you free
Stephen was one of the earliest rebirths, he had no access to God's Word like us. But he had heard the words of Jesus. He had the Torah and some of the prophetic writings. But the most important thing Stephen had was the words he had heard from Jesus and the truth of Jesus' Atonement on Calvary as far as he could understand. and He had also let Jesus become Lord in his life .. He believed this new life's reality and carried

on. We see one of the results of the freedom he seized here.

Peter
We also see Peter at the beautiful temple door. "Peter says. I have no silver or gold, but what I have I give you: In the name of the Nazarene of Jesus Christ - get up and go. " (Acts. 3: 6)

What Peter had gained conviction in his spirit and soul was expressed and became a physical reality.

Filip
We also see Philip coming down to a town in Samaria.

"Then Philip came down to a city of Samaria and preached Christ unto them.

And the people took heed to what was said by Philip, hearing and seeing the signs which he did. " (Acts. 8: 5-6)

Here we see Philip proclaimed and gave freedom from the Lord, which you can do.

We have been given the power to do that has the same efficacy today as it did on Pentecost.

"Jesus said, You shall have power in the coming of the Holy Spirit, and you shall be my witnesses (martyrs, proof-makers) both in Jerusalem and throughout Judea and Samaria and to the ends of the earth." (Acts. 1: 8)

The freedom you have - is the freedom you can give the world
The freedom you have, the freedom of love that God has given you, you can pass on to the world around you. Be Free to set the world free.

2 0

Make the world believe the message - and they will have it

You will make humanity believe the message.

"You shall know the truth, and the truth shall set you free." (John. 8:32)

How is your personal position to face the world?
How is your position face to face with a world that does not know the message of Jesus Christ? Are you able to relate to people living in paganism, occultism, and religions of different kinds? Can you convey the Bible's message to those in a way that makes them receive the message? **Are you able to love these types of people?**

A conqurer of love

Your position above the heathen crowds should be like a conqueror of love.

"As Paul said, you should be able to say: I know who I believe." (2 Tim. 1:12)

Have you gone through so many ups and downs that you can say "I know on whom I believe"?

When you have come to this point in your Christian life, as here Paul has come when he can say "I know who I believe". Then you have gone through many stages of ups and downs, trials and suffering. You have come through these learning processes and forming processes with a steady attachment to the Word of God, which has made you stronger and stronger in the belief in the promises of God's Word in the process. The deeds of the flesh have been distanced more and more from your soul as you live in repentance from the deeds of the flesh. The fruits of the Spirit have come forth and gained control over your soul life more and more. Christ has been given the opportunity to reveal himself more and more to you and through you, to the humanity around you. You have become a Christ person, the love of Christ in you is experienced by everyone around you.

You have become one that can bring the world life
It's the power and love of Christ through you.

"Jesus said, I am the way of truth and life."
(John. 14, 6)

"The devil only comes to steal, murder, and destroy. But I have come to give you life and have an abundance. " (John. 10:10)

You are the one who can turn the power.

What do you see when you see those who have never heard the gospel of Jesus Christ the living Son of God? You see those who seek an unknown God, the one we preach, without knowing that we are preaching that God.

"Paul says: For as I was walking about looking at their shrines, I also found an altar on which was inscribed: To an unknown God. What you

thus cultivate without knowing it, this I proclaim
to you. " (Acts. 17, 23)

The whole world has faith in the resurrected
Christ - that's the limit of the faith they have -
they just don't know it.
Listen to these two Bible verses.

"He has done everything in his day though, also
the eternal (Cosmos) he has put into their hearts,
but so that man cannot fully understand the work
God has done from beginning to end."
(Ecclesiastes 3, 11)

"By grace you are saved, by faith, and it is not of
yourselves, it is the gift of God." (Eph. 2: 8)

"For when the Gentiles, who have not the law,
by nature do what the law command, then these,
though not having the law, are themselves a law;

They show that the work of the law is written in
their hearts, with their conscience also giving
their testimony, and their thoughts among themselves or even defending them" (Rom. 2: 14-15).

"For if you confess with your mouth that Jesus is Lord, and believe in your heart that God raised him from the dead, then you will be saved;" (Rom. 10: 9)

"For their Redeemer is strong, Jesus Christ, he will bring their cause, your cause, the cause of the world, against you, the devil." (Proverbs 23:11)

"For the Lord shall lead, the people, the cause of the world." (Proverbs 22, 23)

The Solver from Calvary

When the world sees you, the new creature, they see "the redeemer from Calvary", it sees "the answer", it sees Christ in you. You know that what you preach, yes, proclaim is the truth, because you have received it yourself. You have become the truth, the truth is in you, Christ is in you.

"Then Philip came down to a city of Samaria, and preached Christ unto them.

And the people gave heed to what was said by Philip, hearing and seeing the signs which he did.

For there were many who had unclean spirits, and those before them with high cries, and many criminals and cripples were healed."
(Acts. 8: 5-8)

Everyone Can Get It This is how I have experienced it all over the world for years. I preach the gospel I believe in strongly. When people see I believe what I proclaim and they see people being set free, they want what I have. The great thing is that what I have is free and everyone can get it. Listen to this.

"A man disfigured from the womb of asking for alms by Peter.

But Peter looked at him sharply with John and said, Look at us!

He then paid attention to them, because he was expecting to get something from them.

But Peter said, I do not own silver and gold; but what I have I give you: In the name of Jesus Christ, the Nazarene, get up and go!
Immediately his feet and ankles gained strength. " (Acts. 3: 1-8)

"Paul said, Yes, I do, and in truth, all for loss, because the knowledge of Christ Jesus, my Lord, is so much more valuable, for whose sake I have suffered loss, and I take it for granted, that I can win Christ. "
(Philip 3: 8-14) Look up and read all the verses.

We are the true "Culturehouse"
We do not need to attend culture courses to reach people in the right way. We are the true "culture house", We fit into any culture with our message.

The "tailor-made" book
We have received the "book" from God, which is "tailor-made" for all people in all cultures. We have a "culture book", the Bible.

Get hooked on the book
Live full of the "culture book", then you become cultural in God's way. We have the message that

reaches all people. It is in us and through us, to those around us.

"Or do you not know that your body is a temple of the Holy Spirit." (1 Cor. 6:19)

"For Christ did not send me to baptize, but to preach the gospel, not in wise words, that the cross of Christ should not lose its power.

The word about the cross is a fool for the lost, but for us who are saved, it is the power of God. " (1 Cor. 1: 17-18)

Paul says in 1 Corinthians 2, 2 - 5 "I would not know anything else among you without Jesus Christ and he crucified.

And I was with you in frailty and in fear and trembling.

And my speech and preaching was not with the persuasive words of wisdom, but with the evidence of spirit and power.

So that their faith should not be based on human wisdom, but on the power of God. "
(1 Cor. 2: 2 - 5)

We can deal with Satan and the demons, but they cannot handle us

Satan and the demons know they must go when we come.

"And when the possessor saw Jesus afar off, he ran and fell down before him,

And cried with a loud voice, What have I to do with thee, Jesus thou Son of the Highest God? I swear to you by God that you must not torment me. " (Mark. 5, 6 - 7)

This is how Satan and the demons see you - a conqueror of love

"The bloodthirsty woman said: If I can touch it, if it is only in his clothes, then I will be healed." (Mark. 5, 28)

This is how the wonderful people of the world
look upon you - such as the faith, the hope,
and the messengers of love.

Love the world and it will love you.
Make the world believe the message and it
wants it.

2 1

You are the messenger of love

How beautiful on the mountains are its feet that come with "glad tidings". Who preaches "peace", who carries "good news", who proclaims "salvation" .... " (Jes. 52: 7)

Isn't this beautifully presented. You know the practical reality of love coming to you just by reading this verse. Imagine meeting this "poet", the proclaimer who comes with the "life" message. Let it be you who comes. We read some Bible sites that confirm this.

The potential for the reborn

" God is love." (1 John. 4: 8)

"God is spirit." (John. 5, 28)

"The love of God is poured out into our hearts by the Holy Ghost." (Rom. 5.5)

Poured into our hearts, "which are the hearts of believers," by the Holy Spirit

"Whoever believes in me, as the scripture has said, of his life shall flow streams of living water." (John. 7, 38)

As you see from this verse, things must be fulfilled, implemented on your part, for this to work for you. It is that we have faith in Christ as Scripture has said. There are clear guidelines for what needs to be done to be born again. When you are born again, you are at the beginning of a whole new life again. This time not in the flesh, but in the spirit.

Here comes the startup manual

Paul gives this to the Romans, hear "If you confess with your mouth Jesus as Lord, and believe in your heart that God raised Him, Jesus from the dead, then you will be saved;" (Rom. 10: 9)

I

Jesus as Lord Jesus must become Lord in your life. He must have complete control over you. He does this by obeying the written Word of God. This takes a long time, but has a beginning. It happens by turning from the past life control systems through the senses and around to the words of Jesus and the Bible.

II

Believe God raised Jesus from the dead This you can believe if you want, everything is controlled with the will power. Read verses I have previously explained, Ecclesiastes 3, 11 and Ephesians 2, 8. These are key verses in this context.

III

You are born again; you are a new creature. If this is in place in your life, then you are born again. You have become a new creation in Jesus Christ. You read this in 2 Corinthians 5, 17. I have referred to it earlier.

The well of love - the well of love is in you
"If you stay in me and my words stay in you, ask
for what you want and you will get it."
(John 15: 7)

You are in love and love is in you.

"If you keep my commandments, you will be in
my love, just as I have kept the Father's commandments and remain in His love."
(John 15:10)

Here we see the "born again" personality that
has begun to fill with the Word of God, which
you must do. What happens when we happen to
you is what happens here. The process of trans-
formation of you is underway, to become Christ
more and more alike.

You are in love - love has become in you.

**Christ did the same for the whole world, as
He did for you**

Let love flow

"Jesus said to the Pharisees, 'You shall love the Lord your God with all your heart and with all your soul and with all your mind.'
This is the greatest and first commandment.

But there is another equally great thing: You must love your neighbor as yourself.

 On these two commandments rests the whole law and the prophets. " (Matt. 22, 37 - 40)

The fruit of verse 37 is verse 39 Your attitude to yourself, what you value in your own life. Nothing else but what you have, as the most important thing in your life, you can pass on. Nothing but what you see and are in yourself.

Dressed up in love

Let the world get itself, as it is meant to be, let it see it in you. You can, by being who you are in Christ, dress in the garments of love.

The prisoners in the prison in Sri Lanka

It shocked me, the reaction I got from five hundred prisoners in prison during and after my message to them in the prison yard. I was interrupted by loud cries of joy and clapping. They shouted we want it; we want what you have.

Love came to me from five hundred prisoners
Love infects, either the same color or the opposite. Those who receive it, those who do not want it, get darker than they have been before. But in the presence of God, they have experienced God's love, hope, joy, enthusiasm and liberating power for all mankind.

" My son! Watch my words, bow your ear to my speech!

Do not let them go from your eyes, keep them deep in your heart!

For they are the life of every one that find them, and the healing of all his body "
(Proverbs 4, 20 - 22)

"Hold on to my targeting, don't let it go! Keep it, because it is your life. " (Proverbs 4: 13)

"Do not let love and faithfulness depart from you, tie them around your neck, write them on your heart's chalkboard!
Then you will find grace and gain good understanding in God and the eyes of men.

Trust in the Lord with all your heart, and do not trust your understanding!

Think of Him in all your ways! Then he will make your paths straight.

Do not be wise in your own eyes, fear the Lord and turn away from evil!

It should be healing for your body and give new strength to your legs. " (Proverbs 3, 3 - 8)

This is your life
What is the value of your life? That is the price Christ paid for you as He gave His life for you in His life's walk on earth and on Calvary's cross, having given His life and blood for the purification of your sins, inheriting the sin that had been with you since you. was born.

"For God so loved the world, that he gave his only begotten Son, that whosoever believeth in him should not perish, but have everlasting life;" (John. 3:16)

Isn't this amazing, you are free if you want to be free. When you understand this, you are revolutionized by the new life. Christ has done the same for you, as he has done for the whole world. Christ gave His life for us in love, so that we will live for Him in the world in love.

Are you happy?
"The joy of the Lord is our strength."
(Neh. 8:10)

Free - to give
"Peter said: What I have, I give you." (Acts 3: 6)

"Jesus said: Is it by the Spirit of God that I cast out the evil spirit, when the kingdom of God is come unto you." (Matt. 12:28)

The kingdom of love
Our values within the Kingdom of God are equal to all who are born again, you just have to inter-

vene, make it yours in Jesus name. Satan will try to prevent you from obtaining everything that is your rights. He cannot do that if you want to take out your rights in Christ.

In the kingdom of love, no one is equal, but everyone has the standard and value of God. God hard the same care for you and everyone else. The great thing about God is that He has more than enough time, always, for each one of us. We will not fully understand this until we are in the heavenly dwellings.

Love is what the world needs - We can't wait any longer
Let the bridge of love heal - Between you and them
Tempt the world forward - Let the world smile - Let it laugh - it deserves it.

2 2

Love your neighbor as yourself

"God shows His love for us in that Christ died for us while we were yet sinners." (Rom. 5: 8)

"For God so loved the world that he gave his only begotten Son, that whosoever believeth in him should not perish, but have everlasting life." (John. 3:16)

How could a God who is pure and perfect love a sinful world?
God had created the earth and all that is on it. God created man as his most excellent creatures. He did it to have something and pour out His Divine love over. Man disobeyed God, but that did not stop God from loving what he had created. He, on the other hand, had to find a solution to bring man back into fellowship with him without the destructive shadows of disobedience.

211

God created man

"And God said, Let us make men in our likeness, according to our likeness; and they shall rule over the fish of the sea, and of the birds of the heavens, and over the cattle, and of all the earth, and of every creeping thing that moves upon the earth.

And God created man in his image, in the image of God he created it; to man and woman he created them.

And God blessed them, and said unto them, Be fruitful, and multiply, and fill the earth, and put it under you, and counsel over the fish of the sea, and over the birds under the heaven, and over every beast that toucheth the earth. "
(Genesis 1, 26)

Man was disobedient to God

"Then God the Lord said to the woman, what have you done? And the woman said, The serpent fooled me, and I ate.
And God said unto the serpent, Because thou hast done this, thou art cursed among all the beasts and of all the beasts. On your belly you

will crawl, and dust you will eat all the days of
your life.

At the same time that God had to give a judgment, God already came here with the solution
for the judgment
But it was not to come until 4000 years later, but
the solution came and man was fully raised,
which God is already talking about here.

"And I will put enmity between you and the
woman, and between your offspring and her offspring; it will crush your head, but you will
crush its heel. " (Gen. 3, 13-15). "

"He raises the lowly of the dust, lifts the poor
from the snare to set him princes and give him
an honorable seat ..." (1 Sam. 2, 8)

"The Lord is exalted above all nations; his glory
is above the heavens.

Who is like the Lord our God, he that thrones so
high,

Who looks so deep, in heaven and on earth,

Who raises the low of the dust, exalts the poor of the cormorant,

To put him in princes, in the princes of his people. " (Psalm 113, 4 - 8)

The solution came in God's only begotten son Jesus Christ
"He who, when he was in the form of God, did not regard it as a prey to be like God,

But of course, he renounced it and took on the form of a servant as he came into the parable of men.

And when he was found as a human being, he humbled himself, so that he became obedient to death, even the death of the cross. " (Phil. 2: 6-8)

The promise came to Abraham after the fall and Christ came with the fulfillment of the promise.

"And the LORD said unto Abraham, I will that thy seed be as the dust of the earth, that one may number the dust of the earth, and that thy seed also may be numbered." (Gen. 13, 16)

What a promise that was then fulfilled in Christ. Jesus opened the door to the new birth of a new kind of people. The God type, the Jesus people, the type of love, the new creature.

"God is love" (1 John. 4, 8)

What we "have" and "are" - we can pass on God could not give anything but what he "is", so it will be with us as new creatures in Christ Jesus. What we "have" and what we "are" we can pass on.

"Beloved, if God has loved us, then we are bound to love one another.

No one has ever seen God, if we love one another, God becomes in us, and the love of Him is perfected in us. " (1 John. 4, 11-12)

God knows we cannot produce love from our soul and spirit until He comes.

"For all that is born of God overcomes the world, and this is the victory that has overcome the world, our faith." (1 John. 5, 4)

"He, Christ, who is the brilliance of his, the glory of God, and the image of his being."
(Heb. 1, 3)

"God is love" (1 John. 4, 8)

"God is spirit" (John. 4, 24)

"Jesus said: You shall love the Lord your God with all your heart (soul and spirit), with all your soul and with all your mind.
This is the first and greatest commandment.

Another that is just as great, you must love your neighbor, like yourself. " (Matt. 22, 37 - 39)

We see love is deep in the Holy Spirit and that is why we must focus. We must focus on the love of God's way; the way God's word prompts us to do so.

Do you love God, do you love yourself, do you love your neighbor?
These are spiritual laws that work.

"Jesus said to the Pharisees, isn't that why you go astray, because you do not know the scriptures, nor the power of God?" (Mark. 12:24)

The Pharisees had enough theological knowledge, but they did not have the necessary, namely, a personal knowledge of the Word of God. This makes the difference of eternity perspective.
Two Different Worlds These are two different worlds, the world of the mind and the world of the Spirit of God. Understanding what God is is and understanding what His words say.

"And do not become like this world, but be transformed by the renewal of your mind ..." (Rom. 12, 2)

"But we who, with an unseen face, behold the glory of the Lord as in a mirror, we are all transformed into the same image from glory to glory, as by the Spirit of the Lord." (2 Cor. 3, 18)

"To sanctify the church, in that he purified it by the water bath in the word ..." (Eph. 5, 26)

In God, you find that you are great and important

Just as important as any other human being on earth. You are the very best of God. The more you get to know the written Word of God, the more you get to know who you are, you learn and live like who you are. Then you will start telling others that they can become who you have become, you tell them that they are just as important as you are.

This is a wonderful message to bring to humanity. If everything has fallen into gravel, then Christ has resurrected us to dignity. When you see your own value, you will love to tell others that they have the same value. Then you are a conqueror in Christ. Your lifestyle has become like a "best of God" - give it to your neighbor. The more you see what you are, the more you can pass on. You cannot save a poor man by being poor - but you can save a poor man by being rich.

People look at themselves negatively and want others to go down with the same negative.

"Don't you know that a little leaven dips all the dough." (1Cor. 5, 6)

Do not accept the leaven of Satan that comes as arrows "Eph. 6: 16)

"And you made him a little inferior to God, with honor and glory you crowned him.

You made Him ruler over the deeds of your hands, everything you put under His feet.
" (Psalm 8, 6 - 7)

You are great, lift others to the same level. As the creation of the greatness of God, the creation of love. You are the one who can do this. Give people the love promise they need.

2 3

Faith Hope and Love

"But now they are standing these three, faith, hope, and love, and the greatest among them is love." (1 Cor. 13:13)

On the mountain of explanation was Peter, Jacob, and his brother John, then this event happens.

"Then Peter answered and said unto Jesus, Lord, it is good for us to be here, If you will, I will make three houses here, one for thee, and one for Moses, and one for Elias.

While he was still speaking, behold, there came the shining cloud, and overshadowed them; behold, a voice came out of the cloud saying, This is my beloved Son, in whom I am well pleased, hear him.

And when the disciples heard it, they fell on their faces and were greatly dismayed.

And Jesus went and touched them, saying, Arise, and be not afraid.

But when they looked up, they saw no one without Jesus alone. " (Matt. 17, 4 - 8)

"Jesus said, I am the way of truth and life."
(John. 14, 6)

Jesus is the way, the truth, and the life, yes he is the reality. One thing is to have knowledge of reality. It is to have the reality, the theology about it. But we must become the reality. It is a necessity if reality is to become real to us, within us and through us to the humanity around us.
It can be

Listen to this Bible word
"Knowledge inflates, but love builds."
(1 Cor. 8: 1)

"But some have been puffed up, thinking that I should not come to you;

But I will come to you soon, and the Lord will, and then learn to know not only the words, but the power of the one who is inflated;

For the Kingdom of God does not consist in words but in power. " (1 Cor. 4, 18-20)

Paul writes to the Philippians
"So that I may know Him and the power of His resurrection and the community of His sufferings, being made equal to Him in His death,

Let us as many as perfect have this mind; and if you are differently minded in something, then God will reveal this to you too;

Just as far as we have come, we continue in the same track! " (Filip 3: 10 and 15 - 16)

You can become a wonderful tool for the kingdom of heaven on earth.

sower
Let's look at the parable of the 4 different "soils". Some were sown by the road, some were sown on rocky ground, some were sown among thorns

and finally, some were sown in good soil. I include a verse from the parable.

"Every time someone hears the word about the kingdom and does not understand it, the evil one comes to rob what is sown in his heart (spirit), this is what was sown by the way." (Matt. 13:19)

The 3 "soils" that lost their lives

There are several important aspects to take from this parable, but I will mention one. Listen to this. All "soils" heard the Word preached. Three of the "soils" got the word robbed from their hearts (spirit) by the evil one, even though they initially received the word. The circumstances of their lives and thinking of the arrows of Satan made them give in. They lost what the Lord had given them. They lost salvation with everything it holds of opportunity.

The good soil

It was a soil that did not yield, but had its eyes fixed on the word of God. The good earth let the word be the first and governing in life, no matter what the circumstances and Satan's arrows said.

God gave us "some more" (Eph 4: 11) - there are no service gifts

I include these Bible sites from Paul's letter to the Ephesians. "Service gift". It is a term that is often used. One can hear questions come as - what service do you have? The correct term is:

He, God Jehovah gave us some ...

"And he gave us some to apostles, some to prophets, some to evangelists, some to shepherds, and teachers,

For the saints (the born-again surrendered) to be consecrated for service, for the edification of the body of Christ,

Until we all reach unity in faith in God's Son and knowledge (not knowledge) to Him, to man's maturity, to the age-goal of Christ's fullness,

That we may no longer be impotent, and let us cast and carry away from every doctrine the teachings of men, by the wisdom of the arts of delusion,

224

But that in truth we believe in love, in every way grow up to Him who is the head, Christ. "
(Eph. 4: 11-15)

I will also include verses that deal with the same in 1 Cor. 12, 28.

"And God first put in the church some apostles, second, prophets, third, teachers, so powerful works, so gifts to heal, to help, to govern, different kinds of tongues." (1 Cor. 12, 28)

Here we see Paul writing it a little differently, he writes, "God put in the church"
In the letter Paul wrote to the Ephesians, "God gave us some" Let's look at what is written here in the Corinthians, "God put in the church."

God put in the church (1 Cor. 12, 28)
First some to apostles.
Secondly, prophets,
Third, teachers (instructor, Greek),
So powerful deeds.
So gracious gifts (plural) to heal,
To help,
To control,

Different kinds of tongues.

Here are mentioned powerful deeds, graces (plural) to heal, Here the shepherd is not mentioned, but "to help", "to govern", "various kinds of tongues".

God gave us some (Eph. 4: 11)
apostles,
some to prophets,
some to evangelists,
someone to shepherd (not a leader in the community, but helps with the "herd" and teacher (instructor, Greek)

I think it is of the utmost importance to be careful in the designation of the various things mentioned here
When it comes to the Lord and His words, the details are important. It is 100% necessary that the knowledge of revelation is present as God wills in the various tasks. Otherwise, it will be a dead proclamation.

NB, NB

Spiritual Leaders and Shepherds as "Commanders and Controllers" in the Church

It is not mentioned anything about this behavior of a Shepherd in the Bible. On the other hand, there are many places in the Bible that we find humility, love, serving minds, and the power of example, to be the qualities in a true Sheperd. Christ himself is the very best example here. Those who want to experience God using them in one of the various tasks I have mentioned, must stand in the right attitude, founded on a surrendered life to Christ Jesus, with the fruits of the Spirit controlling your life.

If not, you're just a destructive factor, no matter how good you are at preaching and capturing people's interest.

We continue with the "sower"

The seed's most important task is to live in revelation knowledge

All the different tasks arranged for the congregation are all "seed" tasks, albeit in slightly different ways. What remains the critical point and the important point for the "sower" is that the sower is a person who has gone God's way with his life, so that as Paul's letter to Gal. 5, 16 - 22 becomes a reality in one's life . It is only when one has gone through these processes of one's life that the knowledge of revelation begins to appear in the character.

The preacher was without revelation and the gate for Satan was open

When "the sower did not understand what he preached, neither did those who heard his preaching understand it." The sowers "preaching" was without revelation. This was the reason why the "soils" that heard the preaching did not understand it, it was without life in it.

That's the reason that Satan could steel

That again was the reason why the evil one could rob what was sown in their hearts. The "soils" wanted what they heard, but they didn't understand. Then came Satan's fiery arrows with manipulative speech and robbed it of them.

Life in the third and the fourth dimension
The fourth dimension – Gods primary dimension of love

This is the Spiritual dimension of Gods Holy Spirit. To be able to live here, you must have a

surrendered, born again spirit filled life with God.
Let's see what Paul's letter to Eph. 3, 17 - 20 says about a life in the 4 dimension, the dimension of the Holy Spirit.

The love dimension, the fourth dimension, Gods Holy Spirit dimension
If you want to live the strong life with God, then this is the place you must come into and forever live in.

"That Christ must dwell by faith in their hearts,

So that you rooted and rooted in love, must be able to understand (understand) with all the saints what breadth and length and depth and height there are,

And know the love of Christ, which transcends all knowledge (sense knowledge), so that you may be filled with all the fullness of God (knowledge of revelation).

But he who can do more than anything, far beyond what we pray or understand, according to the power that works in us, (Eph. 3, 17-20)

The third dimension

In the physical world in which we live in, is a world of three dimensions. In this dimension, we need no more than three measuring units to calculate a physical depth.

Can you see the difference between the third and the fourth dimension?

The Fourth Measuring Unit In the Bible places we just read, we see it mentioned a fourth measuring unit, namely a depth. Here, in the depth, there is a rooting and a "founding in love". Through this attachment, we should then be able to understand the "depth of depth" that the calculation must become. Not just a knowledge of, but an understanding of through revelation.

The 3-dimension Earth is the physical planet we live on, our world is spiritual. The fourth dimension is the spiritual world. Here the Holy Spirit works in the spiritual world. The 4 -dimensions. is meant by Gods Spirit to control this 3 -dimensional planet, the earth.

230

We know this failed – because of Adam and Eve in the garden of Eden

That is why there is to interests in the spiritual world to have control on planet earth and the human beings. Here comes the war in the spirit in the picture.

Knowing the love of Christ that surpasses all knowledge

When we have found the depth of love, which surpasses all knowledge, we have achieved a founding and a rooting of love. These are the door openers into the reality of the spiritual world through the guidance of the Holy Spirit. Here we are talking about the Holy Spirit's knowledge which is stronger and far more com-prehensible than sensory knowledge, human knowledge. Here, wisdom and wisdom are re-ceived from God Jehovah. This is then available to those born again who live their lives surren-dered to Christ according to Bible guidelines. I write more about this in my book "Breakthrough in the World of the Spirit"

Have this in your mind

Listen to this:

"If I have faith so I can move mountains, but do not have love, then I am nothing." (1 Cor 13, 2)

"Whoever does not love does not know God."
(1 John. 4, 7 - 8)

When do you understand this.
We look further.

"Many people will tell me that day. Lord, Lord, we have not spoken prophetically by your name, and cast out evil spirits by your name.
, and done many mighty deeds by thy name.

And then I will testify to them: I have never known you, depart from me, you who did wrong.
" (Matt. 7:22)

The divine love was missing, now you understand this too.

2 4

The Wind of the New Type of Winners The Spiritual Warriors

"The wind blows where it wants to, and you hear it whistle, but you don't know where it comes from and where it leads." (John. 3: 8)

"As little as you know our wind's dangers, or how the bones are formed in the fertile woman's life, as little you know what God wants to do, he who does it all." (Ecclesiastes 11, 5)

"He who leads ... the wind out of his storehouse, treasury." (Psalm 135, 7)

"For as many as are driven by the Spirit of God are the children of God." (Romans 8:14)

"He who has an ear, he heareth what the Spirit saith unto the church (Ecclesia, Greek), he that overcomes." (Rev. 2, 7)

Ecclesia from Greek means, the chosen ones, those who meet/gather in the squares, in Latin Bible translation, Koinonia meaning the community.
If you live your life as a warrior of God, then you must come to the point that God's Spirit can lead your life.

Paul says, "But I say, walk in the Spirit, and ye shall not fulfill the lusts of the flesh (the desire of the senses). For the flesh lusts, lusts against the Spirit, and the Spirit against the flesh, lusts, they oppose one another, lest you do what you will.

If want to live in the Spirit, then let us walk in the Spirit. " (Gal. 5, 16-17)

A life in God's reality
Have you come to the point in your life that you have received and live in an intimate relationship with God's Spiritual reality. You have had a per-

sonal relationship with the Father, the Son, and the Holy Spirit. You live in a reality of the Spirit that is always guided by the written Word of God, the Bible. Whatever spiritual realities you encounter, it will be satanic and demonic, if it does not exactly match the written Word of God, the Bible.

Have you begun to gain experience in this spiritual reality - is your physical life viewed with different eyes? - your world, which is spiritual, but living physically done on earth, will gradually be transformed, because you have been given a different perspective on the reality of life. You and it are transformed because of your knowledge of the spirit world and the Spirit of God in the spirit world. You have consciously begun to move in two dimensions the third dimension and the fourth dimension consciously at the **same time.**

The fourth dimension, the dimension of the spirit, the dimension of God Jave. The dimension of the new type of winner.

**In Paul's letter to the Galatians, we can read about work of the flesh
Read Gal 5, 19 - 22.**

The first serious step to be taken. I we Should be able to gain entrance and communication in the spiritual world? May what you now have read about the deeds of the flesh, and any other things in your life that are not pleasing to God, be reversed. All this have to be repented from, that is a must. This is the first serious step to be taken. It may take some time for this to happen. This is a battle you must win in order to move forward.

Seek God – He has given you a wonderful promise here

If you have been victorious here, you must start seek God, you must seek until you find Him. When you find him, make shure to be with Him allwas and forever. We have this promise of God who take us to the victory, if we want. God says "Whoever seeks me shall find me."

You are now in an unknown area

An area where you have to fight through to victory alone. This can take a long time. I'm not talking about hours, but weeks, yes months. Little by little you will learn what works and what doesn't. Everything that works will always be consistent with the written Word of God, the

Bible. Here is no room for the flesh that will play theater that things are from God. Now we are talking about entering a spiritual world in a real way. Gods spiritual world in the spirit and in the Spirit of God.

Into a world without limits – a never ending world bigger than Cosmos

It costs everything

If you are not willing to bet and let it cost everything it costs you, you will not do it. This is a matter that must be dealt with in your fellowship with God alone. That's what Christianity is about, the relationship between you and Jesus. There is no intermediary here who would be nothing but devastating to you in your daunting relationship with the Trinity of the Godhead.

The Bible is your foundation

"In the beginning was the Word, the Word was with God, and the Word was God." (John. 1, 1)

"And the Word became flesh and dwelt among us, and we saw his glory - a glory which the only begotten Son hath of his Father, full of grace and truth." (John. 1:14)

If you see the connection, you see the greatness, far beyond our understanding
Christ among us in the flesh, as a human being, but bearing God in him, or God in Christ bore him. At the same time, God was out in the spirit world and beyond into the heavenly realms. This is the God of love, his wind is felt everywhere. He created all things, given all kinds of grain in the soil and in the flesh. It is he who makes it grow. It is God's seed of revelation, the watering of revelation that gives the revealed life in all things. That which is of God is always in line with the written Word of God, the Bible. Listen to this Bible verse.

"Jesus said: It is the Spirit that quickens, the flesh helps nothing, the words that I have spoken to you are Spirit and they are life." (John 6, 63)

Jesus went on to say, "For I have come down from heaven, not to do my will, but to do his will that sent me." (John. 6, 38)

We must be the people of the Word, "The people of the book", the book in which the wind of God blows into all things.

"My son, heed my words, bow your ear to my speech!

Do not let them go from your eyes, keep them deep in your heart!

For they are life for everyone that finds them and healing for all his body. Keep your heart above all that is preserved, for life is based on it.
" (Proverbs 4, 20 - 23)
Listen further. "Without revelation, the people perish, but happy is the one who keeps the law, the word of God." (Ecclesiastes 29, 18)

"Peter said, I don't have silver or gold, but what I have I give you." (Acts. 3: 6)

Peter obeyed the word and walked with the Spirit. You can do the same to an even greater extent because we have the written Word of God and two thousand years of experience on the Word of God and take off.

Make them believe it
By the acts of faith, boldness, boldness, toughness, "we experience"

It is at this point the answers to the prayers get a sudden stop. It is tragic to meet Christians who should understand this, but cowardice has caused them to hide the boldness under the rug. They dare not throw up. It can create scratches in pride. Then it is easier to come up with some well-formulated expression from the Bible to try to justify oneself and stop the bold and bold. You hear it: You have to be full of love, you have to show understanding and compassion, you don't have to be so hard. These are common statements from the "unbelieving league."

What do you want? With this kind of attitude, it is completely impossible to get a living bean answering life. A life with God the Father and His son Jesus Christ and guidance through the Holy Spirit. You will automatically gradually fall out of faith. Whoever was born again is no longer, but has ended up as a religious Christian, who thinks everything is fine.
Don't waste your boldness, it has great pay!
(Heb.10, 35)

With great boldness, boldness

"And now, Lord, watch their threats, and give your servants to speak your word with great boldness, boldness, toughness, and wisdom, As you stretch out your hand to healing and to the signs and wonders of your saint, you are serving Jesus' name. " (Acts. 4, 29-30)

Satan's discouragement thoughts

"And if it is a bold man, with a heart like a lion, he will still be discouraged." (2 Sam. 17:10) Satan's thought arrows with despair will always attack you, but we lift the shield of faith with boldness, we never accept Satan's attacks, we know his strategy and go out victorious - always.

Make them believe it - It's victory - always
God bless you.

"In this, my Father is glorified that ye bear much fruit, and ye shall be my disciples. (John 15: 8)

Get ready and fulfill your part of the command.

2 5

Reflection

What I am left with after writing this book is a desire to see the witnesses of God rise up against Satan and the attacks of demons in every place. We find the unbelief and fear in many Christians and it is tragic. The believers' job is not to "work" with the unbelievers and the fearful, then we end up going yonder with the unbelievers. Our job is to get the gospel of conviction and faith out to those who want it, the command we receive from Jesus in Mark 16, 15. This is so thrilling to know from many years of experience and beliefs from the Bible's revelation of the written The Word of God. My wish is for the book to be used as a training book, an instruction book for you, as you do your spiritual training exercises, so that you can become a strong believer with contagious effect and power to the world around you.

"Make them believe it"

In God's Job no. 1 - World Evangelism

Tom Arild Fjeld has traveled the world preaching the gospel since youth. In recent years he has written many books, which now come out in order.

Current books for the time we live in.

Follow on social media, Christian TV stations and newspapers where he has meetings and teaching.

Join and support the service regularly financially, or become a practical partner in it.

Follow the pages and www.twitter.com

Contact tomarildfjeld@gmail.com

Account number: 0532.37.94229

Previously published books by Tom Arild Fjeld

How to receive the miracle of salvation Norwegian, Bulgarian, Romanian, Gassian and English

How to receive the miracle of healing

Reborn (in Romanian)

A New Life (Telegu; Indian Language) Specially written for 40 million Indian Hindu widows.

Books recently published by Tom Arild Fjeld

The Power wins the war

Get a loose box (Norwegian and English)

The hidden world

Dress up for victory

A warrior for Christ

Impact in the spirit world

Victory over Satan

At the Barricade

More than one conqueror

Really free

Go out into the world

He gave his life - nobody could take it (Norwegian, English)

The Divine Realities

1 Daily breakthrough (3 months)

2 Daily breakthrough (3 months)

244

3 Daily Breakthrough (3 months)
4 Daily breakthrough (3 months)